"Kristen has offered Christian [...] saturated gift in this book! She [...] of redemption with frank and realistic engagement with today's youth culture and its dangers, and does so conversationally and winsomely. As a pastor/chaplain to high school and college students for the last ten years and now a father to daughters of my own, I commend this book to you as a solid resource for guiding young women toward an unshakeable identity that is grounded in the promises of a good and gracious God."

Jon Nielson, Author of *Gospel-Centered Youth Ministry* and *Faith That Lasts: Raising Kids Who Don't Leave the Church*

"*Face Time* offers an age-old solution to a current crisis. Today's teenagers are the first generation of people to live their entire life with exposure to social media. Today's parents are the first to have to consider how to handle the new challenges that technology is presenting. At the end of the day, the underlying problems come down to the same, eternal human problem: our desire to manufacture our own worth and build our own righteousness. Kristen Hatton offers a wise, smart, and helpful direction on how the gospel of grace offers comfort, freedom, and life in light of these issues. This book is a life-line for so many people who experience fear and desperation around these issues."

Cameron Cole, Chairman of Rooted: Advancing Grace-Driven Ministry; director of youth ministries, Cathedral Church of the Advent, Birmingham, AL; coeditor, *Gospel-Centered Youth Ministry*

"Our sense of identity guides the many conscious and unconscious decisions we make. It's the lens through which we see the world. So it shouldn't be a shock that when our sense of identity becomes unhealthy, our life has a tendency to follow. Each chapter of *Face Time* gives us an insight into a specific lie that can infiltrate our identity and damage our sense of self. When we are able to root out these lies and get to the truth that lies beneath, we are on the path to a happier, healthier life."

Jonathan Steingard, Lead singer for Hawk Nelson

"As a woman, mom, friend, and former teenage girl herself, Kristen Hatton understands the intense pressure and devastating effects of trying to measure up in a constantly changing culture. With compassion and clarity, she offers wisdom that is deeply rooted in God's Word and God's character. She offers practical help and real hope as she shows the reader how to find the freedom that comes only through an identity in Christ."

Courtney Doctor, Director of Women's Ministry at Kirk of the Hills, PCA; author of *From Garden to Glory*

"The depression rate in teens has been linked to the ever-increasing usage of social media, making *Face Time* most timely in the realm of both Christian and professional counseling. Kristen's book provides spiritual depth and truth to addictive behaviors like body image, eating disorders, and self-injury that plague hurting adolescents and adults alike. It's time to turn off the screen and dive into a book that reminds the soul of its true identity and worth."
Alice H. Churnock, Licensed Professional Counselor; Certified Eating Disorder Specialist

"Kristen's words offer a 'me too' for young women to know and understand that they aren't the only ones who deal with the comparison game that social media often presents. She breathes life into the identity of young women and reminds them that no amount of likes, comments, or validation through Instagram can satisfy the way the fierce love of the Lord can!"
MacKenzie Wilson, Founder and Creative Director, Delight Ministries

"As a mom with two girls, one in middle school and one in college, Kristen's fresh perspective brings hope to the struggles girls experience from our social media and selfie-driven world. Through the constant struggles of inadequacy, distorted desires, and obsession with appearance and performance, *Face Time: Your Identity in a Selfie World*, offers girls a gospel-centered solution to the 'identity crisis' currently consuming our distracted and disconnected culture. Kristen equips young believers with the truth of God's acceptance and encourages them to embrace who he created them to be in Christ Jesus. Her personal experiences and creative illustrations will captivate and inspire girls to look *up* to Jesus rather than looking at all that surrounds them. Thank you, Kristen, for impacting this generation of girls for Jesus. I can't wait to get a copy for my girls!"
Annie Pajcic, Founder of ThouArtExalted Ministries, www.thouartexalted.com

"Kristen Hatton's passion to see the beauty and freedom of Jesus's sacrifice grow in the hearts of teenage girls couldn't possibly be more evident. Clearly a labor of love, *Face Time* invites teenagers to engage their lives with an idolatry and identity framework rooted in the gospel. Hatton provides realistic and relatable stories for girls to find themselves in and offers insightful questions to help them exegete their lives and culture."

Liz Edrington, Coordinator of Girls' Discipleship and Young Adults at North Shore Fellowship; counselor at Summit Counseling Center, Chattanooga, TN

"As a father of teens, I often feel overwhelmed and ill-equipped with the changes that social media is making in our everyday lives. Kristen Hatton has provided a huge dose of information, wisdom, and gospel-oriented encouragement in this book. I highly recommend it."

Michael Horton, J. Gresham Machen Professor of Theology, Westminster Seminary California; author of *Core Christianity*; cohost of the *White Horse Inn*

"We've long since passed a time when socialization of our children was the limited domain of families, churches, and schools. By their teenage years our children face an array of influences, not the least being the pervasive and growing impact of social media. Kristen Hatton has written a wise, winsome, and biblically informed road map to help girls navigate an online culture that can create enormous pressure and anxiety. Highly recommended."

Tom Cannon, National Coordinator, Reformed University Fellowship

"As I read *Face Time*, I thought of adult women I've discipled who've struggled with similar pain and sin as the teen girls highlighted in this book. How might their faith and lives have been impacted had they read *Face Time* when they were younger? I recommend this book for every 'little woman' and those who love and disciple them. *Face Time* is the gospel-filled, wisdom-rich book I've longed to see written!"

Ellen Dykas, Women's Ministry Director, Harvest USA; author of *Sexual Sanity for Women: Healing from Sexual and Relational Brokenness* and *Sex and the Single Girl: Smart Ways to Care for Your Heart*

FACE TIME

Your Identity in a Selfie World

Kristen Hatton

WWW.NEWGROWTHPRESS.COM

New Growth Press, Greensboro, NC 27404
www.newgrowthpress.com

Cover Design: Faceout Books, faceoutstudio.com
Typesetting: Lisa Parnell, lparnell.com

ISBN: 978-1-942572-99-2 (Print)
ISBN: 978-1-942572-88-6 (eBook)

Library of Congress Cataloging-in-Publication Data

Names: Hatton, Kristen, 1972– author.
Title: Face time : your identity in a selfie world / Kristen Hatton.
Description: Greensboro, NC : New Growth Press, 2017. | Includes
    bibliographical references.
Identifiers: LCCN 2017002636 | ISBN 9781942572992 (trade paper)
Subjects: LCSH: Teenage girls–Religious life. | Teenage girls–Conduct of life. |
    Christian teenagers–Religious life. | Christian teenagers–Conduct of life. |
    Identity (Psychology)–Religious aspects–Christianity. | Identity (Psychology)
    in adolescence.
Classification: LCC BV4551.3 .H38 2017 | DDC 248.8/33–dc23
LC record available at https://lccn.loc.gov/2017002636

Printed in Canada

24 23 22 21 20 19 18 17   1 2 3 4 5

DEDICATION

To my precious little nieces: Cate, Linley, and Margaret,

May the present joy of your childhoods be preserved through knowing your infinite value and true identity, secure in the work and worth of Christ for you.

Contents

Foreword

I remember being a teenage girl. Yes, it was a long, long time ago but I do remember. I remember the angst, the insecurity, and the pain. I remember sitting in my parents' bedroom, crying to my mom about feeling left out, feeling less than all the other girls. Those feelings plague me even now, but to a lesser degree, praise God. (Although my mom still has to listen to me when they mount a sneak attack.)

I have a teenage daughter. I see those same feelings making an unwelcome appearance in her life as well. I recognize their mark with every heartbreak, every downcast look. Being a teenage girl is harder now than it has ever been. Social media, while not evil in and of itself, has raised the stakes and made the temptations to angst, insecurity, and pain a click away. While those temptations raged in social settings when I was a teenager, I could go home, where they didn't follow me—there was a break from the siren call. But now there is no break. Now the siren calls day and night from smart phones and computers. Our girls are in the fight for their lives. Their identity is threatened at every turn. The fight for each of us to find where we fit in this world is a grueling one that will not end until we see Jesus face to face. We need weapons for the battle. We need hope to go on. We need courage to face another day when the same fears beleaguer us. Our only hope is the gospel, the good news of the life, death, and resurrection of Jesus Christ. The news that our identity doesn't have to be tied up in how we look, how we perform, or how we have failed to perform. This message isn't just relevant for teenage girls, but for everyone reading this book.

We are all—every one of us, from grandmother to teenage girl—looking to find our identity, our place. The real problems come when we fail at this endeavor—and mind my words when I say that, outside of Christ, we will *always* fail at this endeavor. When we forget the gospel (or perhaps we have never heard how Christ's work has changed everything for us), we will end up despairing or proud. When our misplaced hope for identity building is revealed as the faulty savior that it is, where do we turn? Where do our girls turn? When any one of us doesn't get the likes or the comments we wanted, either on social media or IRL, where do we turn to find comfort and hope? Sometimes we double down on our efforts to look prettier or more capable; sometimes we give up completely, sinking headlong into depression; and sometimes we pursue pleasure in the tangible.

The road to self-salvation is always a road to self-destruction. We must have an identity gifted to us. We must have something outside ourselves to save us. Only God himself is able to take all of our efforts to clean ourselves up and show us how worthless they are and yet, at the same time, show us how valuable we are to him. He has loved us with an everlasting love, before we ever did anything right or wrong. Only God himself is able to take all of our desperate attempts to anesthetize the pain of not being good enough and gently lift our faces to him. He causes his face to shine upon us and give us peace.

Kristen Hatton understands the importance of helping our girls find their identity in that good news. She understands it so well that she has poured her heart into these pages. She is a mom to three teenagers and has watched grace transform her parenting and her children's lives. Throughout the pages of this book, you will be shocked at how the gospel really does apply to every situation. Like a skillful surgeon, she delves into situation after situation that a teenage girl might encounter and applies the healing balm of the gospel. The really excellent part is she doesn't just dress the wounds and send you away, happily ignorant of how she did it. She shows *you* how to dress the wounds of false identity as well. I am grateful to walk and work alongside her.

My encouragement to you, as you read this book with your teenage daughter or with a girl you are mentoring, is that you would not just apply the gospel to her life, but that you would apply it to yourself. My prayer is that you and whoever you read this book with would grow in your obsession for Jesus. If you are a teenage girl who has picked up this book on your own, be prepared to have your life changed and your eyes opened to the beauty of Jesus Christ, your friend, your brother, and your Savior, who gave himself up for you to redeem you.

Jessica Thompson

Introduction

When I get a lot of comments, likes, or re-tweets on a picture or post, I feel . . .

Special. Supreme. Better. Popular. Proud.

When my pictures or posts don't get the responses I desire, I feel . . .

Upset. Disappointed. Worried no one likes me. Not as interesting, witty, or pretty. Ugly. Lonely. Not Cool. Deflated. Like I should delete it because it isn't good enough.

The reason I feel like I don't measure up to my friends is because . . .

Their personalities, looks, and talents overshadow mine. My life seems so boring. They are prettier, skinnier, or richer.

In my opinion, the biggest issues teens are faced with are . . .

Pressure to be perfect. Judgment. Trying to measure up. Stress.

To cope with stress, depression, or the way I am feeling, I have . . .

Binged. Purged. Restricted food. Abused alcohol. Used tobacco or drugs. Cut or burned myself. Been sexually active.

I cannot talk to my friends about these things because . . .

I don't want them to know I'm struggling or feeling that insecure.

I cannot talk to my parents about these things because . . .

They won't understand. They will get mad at me. I don't want them to worry.

If these comments resonate with you, you are definitely not alone. These are just a sampling of the responses made by teenage girls to questions in an informal, online survey I developed to understand the effects of social media.

Whether it's Instagram, SnapChat, Twitter, Facebook or whatever new platform takes their place, social media constantly exposes you to what others are doing, how they look, and who they are with. For many habitual users of social media, this quickly leads down the destructive path of feeling less-than, as if they don't measure up to those around them. As the pressure to be perfect mounts and their own perceived failures are magnified, it doesn't take much to fall prey to self-pity, discontent, and depression. Even if this is not your experience, it's unlikely that you have escaped the comparison game completely. Perhaps you find yourself on the other end of the spectrum, feeling as if you are winning the comparison competition because of how you look, what you have, or who you hang out with. But that has traps of its own, and you may have encountered some of them already.

I came up with the online survey when I discovered how social media had contributed to my own daughter's false sense of worth. To be honest, I was caught off guard when I learned about her intense struggles with inadequacy. She'd always come across as confident, beautiful, popular, and successful. When I discovered that she felt like she was anything but that, it made me wonder if others who looked like they had it all together felt the same way she did.

My survey was informal and not associated with any scientific study. But as responses from other teenage girls came in, it confirmed that my daughter was not alone in her struggle. I was blown away by the number of teenage girls across the country, from big cities and small towns, in public school, private school, and home school environments, who expressed similar sentiments. I was filled with sadness, not just about the way technology does so much to encourage a distracted, disconnected culture, but about the deeper problems at the root of the more visible struggles that teenagers (and adults) experience.

Not feeling secure, valued, worthy, loved, accepted, or understood has led teenagers (and adults) to seek security, value, worth, love, and acceptance in sources that can never fully satisfy—nor are they meant to. Many of the things we try in order to feel better about ourselves lead nowhere and often only intensify our struggle. But when we are seeking to find our identity in them, it's hard to turn away. The responses that teenage girls shared with me confirmed that a lot of problem behaviors have their roots in an identity crisis.

As a Christian, I believe that only Jesus can provide the deep security, value, worth, love, and acceptance we all long for. But I know that it's sometimes hard to see what that looks like and how to find it. That is why I've written this book. If you've been struggling with an identity crisis of your own— and maybe some behaviors and thoughts that intensify it—I hope you will find great hope in reading it. I hope, first, that you'll see you are not alone and, second, that you'll discover how to rest in your true identity, found only in him.

Part I shows how the foundation of our brokenness goes all the way back to Adam and Eve. From then on, all humanity has been searching to be filled and made right. So, no matter what you are going through, you are not alone. Your struggles may look different from the next person's, but all of us have hearts that are lost, wandering, and wishing for more.

Jesus saw all the brokenness that came through Adam and Eve and came to earth to heal our hearts and make things right. He entered into our humanness, so he understands what we go through; in fact, he suffers alongside us. He is a God of compassion, who loves us despite our mess, despite the choices we've made that have made things worse, despite our failures and the ways we've done wrong. He loved us so much that he was willing to experience his Father's rejection at the cross, so that he could take the punishment our sins deserved and his perfection could be credited to us. The cross of Jesus is where we find our security, true value and worth, real comfort, and ultimate contentment. I'll show you how those two things fit together.

After seeing who Jesus is for us and how that impacts who we are and how we see ourselves, Part II will show how these truths apply to some common issues that teen girls struggle with. You may relate to some of the stories yourself, while you may recognize others as the struggles of a friend. Each chapter is meant to help you figure out where the girl in the story has missed the connection between her struggles and the promises that God has made to her through the gospel. You'll think about how her situation would change if she better understood her identity in Christ. Ultimately, Part II is meant to help expose the empty things that are so easy to trust in as sources of security and life—false saviors, really—and lead you to trust more fully in the One who truly is life. And as you understand these struggles better, I think it will increase your compassion for those around you.

This book can be read on your own or adapted for a small group study. Discussing the chapters, stories, and questions with others in a safe environment may help you take in the truths in a deeper way. Whether you are currently treading water emotionally, sinking under the weight of your struggles, or trying to soar in your own strength, my prayer for you is that this book will help you see your need for the good news of Jesus Christ. When you see who he is and what he has done for you, you can experience who you are with confidence, peace, and contentment.

PART I:

. . . .

Your True Identity

Chapter 1
Our Selfie World Reality

Meredith is well known and well liked in her large high school. She plays volleyball, serves as an officer in Student Council and the Honor Society, and still manages to babysit for several families who adore her. On top of that, she looks gorgeous and is always beautifully dressed. Ask anyone who knows her: She is perfect.

So when Meredith talked about her life at a large student ministry retreat, her peers were stunned to learn that an intense struggle with self-image had led her down the path to an eating disorder.

How could Meredith have struggled with her self-worth when she had everything going for her?

This was Holly's question as she listened to Meredith speak. Holly struggled with the same things, but she'd assumed that someone like Meredith would never have the problems she did. After all, her family life was nothing like Meredith's, and she wasn't nearly as pretty, popular, or involved at school. Although she was a little nervous to confide in someone she barely knew, Holly decided to text Meredith to thank her for sharing what she did and to share her own struggles. Because each was willing to be vulnerable, a new, unexpected friendship blossomed between the two girls.

As Emma scrolled through her social media feed Sunday evening, she felt more and more depressed. In every picture her friends were literally perfect. Why couldn't she be them? Her life was so boring compared to theirs. Besides seeing plans she had been left out of, she also noticed how many more "comments" and "likes" everyone else received on their photos. "I need to delete my post," Emma thought. "I'll just look like a loser if I don't get more 'likes.'"

Caroline was scrolling through social media that same Sunday night after a full weekend of fun. She couldn't decide which of her pictures to post; she wanted to make sure it wasn't the same one another friend had already posted. But she needed to decide quickly, as she knew it was important to post at just the right time to get the most "likes." Typically, she got hundreds within minutes, which gave her great satisfaction. She loved the attention and had become dependent on it for self-confidence boosts.

For Emma and Caroline, social media was the way they determined how they compared to their peers. While their experiences were different, their hearts were the same. They both desperately wanted to know they were okay.

Can you relate?

Have you experienced feelings like Meredith's, Holly's, Emma's, or Caroline's?

Do you find yourself comparing yourself to others, trying to determine where you measure up and where you don't?

Have you felt isolated or alone, thinking that your parents wouldn't understand and your friends don't have the same problems as you do?

Guess what?

You are not alone! We are all in the same boat. Believe it or not, every one of us is broken and struggling.

Whether you look like you have it all together or you know you don't, whether you have lots of friends or feel like you don't have any, whether your family is intact or barely functioning, you can be sure that your peers are experiencing many of the same insecurities and thoughts. The struggles will look different from person to person, but because there is an underlying desire in each of us to be accepted, we all struggle.

I've talked with a lot of teens and conducted an informal, online survey[1] that made the reality of our similar struggles very clear. Among the things I discovered:

- **Almost 75 percent of the teens surveyed struggle with comparing themselves to others, whether on social media, at school, a social event, or elsewhere.**
- **Over 50 percent don't feel like they measure up to their friends. They view their friends as prettier, more popular, wealthier, better dressed, more fun, or just plain cooler in the way they act.**
- **Fifty percent have felt stressed or depressed because they do not measure up.**
- **Fifty percent feel a very high level of stress from the pressure to be perfect at everything.**
- **The majority of those surveyed say they feel alone and cannot talk to their parents about what they are experiencing. Nearly 50 percent say they cannot share openly with their friends.**
- **Even friends are often viewed as unsafe to talk to because survey respondents fear they will be judged, misunderstood, or not taken seriously. They question whether their friends can be trusted or would even care.**
- **Half of the teens said they would change something about their appearance if they could; the other half wish they could change something about their personality or abilities.**
- **Almost everyone feels things must be perfect for them to be happy.**

Whoa! Those numbers represent a generation of struggling teenagers and young adults. It's likely that you identify with these survey responses and your peers do too, whether you think they have it all together or not. My guess is that they, like you, may at times feel alone in their thoughts, afraid to be vulnerable and honest even with friends.

Have you seen The CW show "Gossip Girl," based on Cecily von Ziegesar's popular young adult novels? With just one episode, it is apparent that every teen (and adult) character in the show is afraid to be truly known. They hide the reality of their lives and feelings behind the mask of apparently perfect, privileged lives. No one knows how badly the others are hurting. Even girls who are supposedly best friends hold deep secrets and hostility toward each other. Everyone uses the others to get what they want. Though they feign happiness, in one telling scene a teen boy admits to another, "Happiness does not seem to be on the menu." While the characters may fool each other, it is clear to the viewer that they are all alone and struggling in similar ways.

If you are anything like me, you are asking, why do so many people struggle this way? How does it happen and— even more importantly—how can we change?

Social media, with the endless competition and comparisons it encourages, intensifies our struggle with self-esteem or, as I prefer to call it, our sense of our own worth. But our problems didn't start with social media or the culture we live in. And, while eliminating social media or isolating ourselves from our surroundings may lessen the intensity of our negative self-talk, it won't solve the struggles we have at the heart level, the identity level, or the "Who am I and what am I worth?" level.

Without realizing it, we tie our worth to our appearance and performance. How we feel about ourselves rises and falls, based on how we look, how well we do (or don't do) at any given task, and how we think others perceive us. So when we think we look good, feel good, and perform well compared to those around us, we feel better about ourselves. But when we assume that everyone else is doing better than we are, we feel as if our value is diminished.

Wouldn't it be nice to view someone else's post without it affecting your mood? Do you think it's possible to feel genuinely happy, not threatened, when you read about another's accomplishments? Is it possible for the twinge of jealousy *not* to bubble up inside you when your friend gets compliments for how gorgeous she looks?

What would it take to be so secure that other people's looks have no impact on you? Can you imagine going through life feeling at peace with who you are? Maybe you can't right now, or maybe you do feel okay today, but you fear that the security is fleeting. I hope that over the next few chapters you will see that, no matter what your unique situation, back story, or struggles, you can find rest in who you are and know your infinite value and true identity in Christ.

REFLECTION TIME

1. How do you identify with the information compiled in the survey?
2. How does it help to hear that other teens feel alone the way you do? If it does not help, why?
3. Why do you think people don't talk about their struggles or feelings?
4. Are you able to confide in a friend about your struggles or feelings? Why or why not?
5. Why do you think we all have these struggles?
6. Does reading this chapter give you hope that you can live differently?

LAST LOOK AND JOURNALING

Read the verses below and then use the space to reflect on the emptiness of what we look to for significance and "life," compared to the true hope we have for something better.

Job 15:31 | Ecclesiastes 2:1–11 | Isaiah 57:13 | 1 Peter 1:3–4

· ·
· ·
· ·
· ·
· ·
· ·
· ·
· ·
· ·
· ·
· ·
· ·
· ·
· ·
· ·
· ·
· ·
· ·
· ·
· ·

Why do you think we all struggle the way we do? We know how we feel, we know what we think we need, but no matter what we do to try to fix ourselves, it doesn't work—at least not long-term. So we keep trying and trying to get what we think will make us feel okay about ourselves.

The limited understanding we have of our own hearts and needs is a pretty good indication that we need help outside ourselves. And the truth is, that's the way we were made. Sadly, our first parents, Adam and Eve, rejected the notion that we were created to live dependent on God. They set all humanity on a course that, believe it or not, is responsible for the identity struggles you face today. Those struggles are part of a much bigger problem that the Bible calls sin and our alienation from God. Let's look at Genesis, the book of beginnings, to see the roots of the problems we all face. You may find it much more relevant to your identity problems than you initially think.

In the first two chapters of Genesis, the Lord created the world and proclaimed everything as "good." Adam and Eve were created to reflect the perfect image of God and to live in a perfect relationship with him and with each other. They (and we) were made to be relational beings, created to know God and to find their meaning, purpose, and value through him.

It started out wonderfully. I imagine Adam and Eve being captivated with each other, totally free to trust each other and be themselves in each other's presence. And that was true in their relationship with God as well! Not only that, but they lived in the spectacular beauty of their garden home, with a great, fulfilling purpose in overseeing it all. All really was bliss.

But then we move to Genesis 3. We are immediately alerted to the evil presence of an unholy intruder (Satan) into the garden, an intruder whose every slithering movement is in total defiance of God and his authority. An intruder so repulsed by God and the glory of the garden that he concocts a plan to lead God's image-bearers to forsake God as the one they look to for meaning, life, purpose, and identity. Satan's true aim was to separate us from God and to usurp God's authority so that *he* can reign over creation. Keep that in mind as you carefully read this passage.

Genesis 3:1–22

[1] Now the serpent [Satan] was more crafty than any other beast of the field that the LORD God had made. He said to the woman, "Did God actually say, 'You shall not eat of any tree in the garden'?" [2] And the woman said to the serpent, "We may eat of the fruit of the trees in the garden, [3] but God said, 'You shall not eat of the fruit of the tree that is in the midst of the garden, neither shall you touch it, lest you die.'" [4] But the serpent said to the woman, "You will not surely die. [5] For God knows that when you eat of it your eyes will be opened, and you will be like God, knowing good and evil." [6] So when the woman saw that the tree was good for food, and that it was a delight to the eyes, and that the tree was to be desired to make one wise, she took of its fruit and ate, and she also gave some to her husband who was with her, and he ate. [7] Then the eyes of both were opened, and they knew that they were naked. And they sewed fig leaves together and made themselves loincloths.

[8] And they heard the sound of the LORD God walking in the garden in the cool of the day, and the man and his wife hid themselves from the presence of the LORD God among the trees of the garden. [9] But the LORD God called to the man and said to him, "Where are you?"

¹⁰ And he said, "I heard the sound of you in the garden, and I was afraid, because I was naked, and I hid myself." ¹¹ He said, "Who told you that you were naked? Have you eaten of the tree of which I commanded you not to eat?" ¹² The man said, "The woman whom you gave to be with me, she gave me fruit of the tree, and I ate." ¹³ Then the Lord God said to the woman, "What is this that you have done?" The woman said, "The serpent deceived me, and I ate."

¹⁴ The Lord God said to the serpent, "Because you have done this, cursed are you above all livestock and above all beasts of the field; on your belly you shall go, and dust you shall eat all the days of your life. ¹⁵ I will put enmity between you and the woman, and between your offspring and her offspring; he shall bruise your head, and you shall bruise his heel."

¹⁶ To the woman he said, "I will surely multiply your pain in childbearing; in pain you shall bring forth children. Your desire shall be for your husband, and he shall rule over you."

¹⁷ And to Adam he said, "Because you have listened to the voice of your wife and have eaten of the tree of which I commanded you, 'You shall not eat of it,' cursed is the ground because of you; in pain you shall eat of it all the days of your life; ¹⁸ thorns and thistles it shall bring forth for you; and you shall eat the plants of the field. ¹⁹ By the sweat of your face you shall eat bread, till you return to the ground, for out of it you were taken; for you are dust, and to dust you shall return."

²⁰ The man called his wife's name Eve, because she was the mother of all living. ²¹ And the Lord God made for Adam and for his wife garments of skins and clothed them. ²² Then the Lord God said, "Behold, the man has become like one of us in knowing good and evil . . . ."

Did you see how Satan pulled off his plan? He began by encouraging Eve and Adam to distrust God's words and his love for them. He persuaded them to violate the one command God had given them, which was not to eat of the "tree of the knowledge of good and evil" (Genesis 2:16–17). Adam's obedience was God's condition for life and blessing, but when Satan whispers to Eve, "Did God actually say, 'You shall not eat of any tree in the garden?'" (Genesis 3:1) she begins questioning God and his goodness. "Surely, we won't die!" She is no longer trusting God for her life, her identity, and her purpose. She has taken a step towards independence—but not a healthy kind that trusts the One who loved her and made her, but one based on doubt and discontent.

Her independent thinking is all Satan needs to push a little further. "You will not surely die. For God knows that when you eat of it your eyes will be opened, and you will be like God, knowing good and evil" (Genesis 3:4).

In plain terms what Satan said is, "Come on, woman! God doesn't want you to eat from this tree because he doesn't want you to become like him. He is withholding something good from you. He is lying when he said 'You will surely die.'"

By portraying God as one who withholds good things from his children so that no one can share his spotlight, Satan presents God as the evil one and himself as the one with Adam and Eve's best interests in mind.

Now, Adam and Even had no reason to doubt God's love, loyalty, and promise to bless them. He literally had just given them the world! This is why their response is so astonishing. Instead of responding in shock to Satan's attack on God's authority, word, and character, the words of the serpent opened Eve's eyes to a new version of reality. At that moment, what Eve *perceived* to be true held more weight than the truth and authority of God's word and all that he had done for them and given them. The once-forbidden tree she now saw as good and she defiantly ate from it.

We might say that Eve is the first relativist; she sees herself as the ultimate judge of reality and truth. She may be the first relativist, but she's certainly not the last. Don't we often do the same thing? We decide what's true based on what we see and think, not on what God's Word says to be true. Even if what we see is nothing more than a filtered Instagram picture, it can carry more weight in determining how we view ourselves than what God says about who we are.

When Adam and Eve decided to eat the fruit, they were deciding that they knew better than their Creator God. What they thought they saw blinded them to the reality of God's lavish love. So instead of acting as God's image-bearers by rejecting the serpent, Adam and Eve chose to align themselves with Satan.

They rejected God's rule in a desire to be their own gods, their own ultimate authority. This choice caused the honor and dignity bestowed upon man and woman by God to be distorted. Without knowing what they were doing, they chose separation from God, insecurity, and brokenness for themselves and for all who followed them. They opened up the world to sin, death, and destruction.

As we look at this tragedy, Adam and Eve's foolishness seems so clear. Yet their foolishness, blindness, and self-focused independence live on in us. Just like Adam and Eve, we want to be our own god. We ignore and reject God's goodness and grace, as we too believe that our plan for our lives is better than God's. We think we know what we need, and we want to go after it in our own way.

One of the most tragic things about Eve's desire to be like God was that she was blind to the fact that she had *already* been made like God—in his image! Only Satan deceived her into thinking otherwise. If Adam and Eve had trusted and obeyed God and stayed away from the tree of the knowledge of good and evil, the tree of life would have brought God's promised blessing that they would be perfected in his likeness. But once they chose disobedience, God's image in them was like a broken mirror—cracked, though not completely destroyed.

Now, Adam and Eve were no longer naked and unashamed (Genesis 2:25). Instead of being secure and content in who God had made them to be, they saw their sin and were ashamed, in the presence of God and each other. They no longer saw the perfect reflection of God in each other. In an attempt to hide their guilt and shame, they sewed fig leaves together to cover themselves. But in those efforts, they reflected the image of the one who had led them astray.

When God came in to the garden to question them, they answered with the kinds of half-truths and blame shifting they had learned from Satan. Because they now reflected Satan's deceitful character, they could no longer remain in God's presence. Their perfect relationship with God was lost, and they were banished from the garden because of their sin.

Adam and Eve's sin has had life-altering consequences for all of mankind. Genesis 3 is not just Adam and Eve's story, but our story too. As historical figures, Adam and Eve were the representatives for the whole human race. Through their rebellion, sin entered the world and corrupted us all, separating us from God. We inherited a sinful nature that no longer naturally loves and trusts God. Instead, like Eve, we buy into lies and are led astray. We want to control our own lives and to be our own authority. And we live as if we are the center of the universe.

Yet living like this is exhausting, because it is not how we were created. We look to others for the approval that Adam and Eve had once known fully in God. We hide behind masks because we are afraid that if people really saw us as we are, they would reject us. Our insecurity has a cruel side too. Our need to see ourselves as better than others leads us to despise those who don't treat us the way we want to be treated. We judge those we think are beneath us. We sometimes even forsake our friends if we think someone or something else can offer us more. We fight against anything that keeps us from what we want or think we must have.

This is a depressing reality check about ourselves, but Genesis 3 also includes God's first words about his promise to bring us back to himself. The most important part of the chapter is not the sin that ruined the world but God's plan to restore and rebuild what was broken.

When Adam and Eve ate the fruit, they did not die, even though this is what they deserved. God postponed his judgment and instead subjected the world to the death, pain, sorrow, suffering, disunity, discord and conflict we cannot escape in this life. But these pains are temporary.

By delaying judgment, God set in motion his plan to save people from what their sin deserves. He would send a redeemer who would take the punishment for our sin and restore us as his image-bearers. But to be restored, we need to know how desperately we need rescuing.

The troubles that began in Genesis 3 help us understand why we think, act, and feel the way we do. We get an overall understanding of the nature of evil, temptation, and sin, and why the world is the way it is. On a personal level, the chapter sheds light on the struggles we talked about in chapter 1: Why we struggle to love and forgive others, why we have relational conflict, why we long to be loved by others, why we fear others knowing who we really are, and why we seek after things other than God. It's a dark story, and not at all flattering. But it's not the end of the story. There is hope ahead.

REFLECTION TIME

1. Why is it important to understand what happened when Adam and Eve sinned?
2. Why do you think it is good for us to know the true condition of our hearts?
3. As you read Genesis 3, did your view of God change? Why or why not?

4. What voice determines truth for you: your own, your peers, culture, God's Word? Why?
5. What makes submitting to God's authority hard for you?

LAST LOOK AND JOURNALING

Use the space below to reflect on what you see about our human condition from this chapter and the verses below.

Genesis 6:5 | Mark 7:20–23 | Romans 3:10 | Ephesians 2:1–3

· ·

· ·

· ·

· ·

· ·

· ·

· ·

· ·

· ·

· ·

· ·

· ·

· ·

· ·

In the last chapter, we talked about Genesis 3 to better understand how we got to feeling so insecure, anxious, jealous, and alone. As we looked at how sin and separation from God entered the human story and every human heart, we saw the roots of our struggles with identity and a positive self-image. True, the explanation was not exactly what we want to hear, but that was not the end of the story, not in the garden of Eden, and not in your life.

Whatever your story, whatever you are going through, whatever you are struggling with, whatever makes you worry, feel hopeless or depressed, it's time to take another look at Genesis 3 to learn about the One who was promised.

After God questioned Adam and Eve in the garden, he turned his attention to the serpent saying, "I will put enmity between you [Satan] and the woman, and between your offspring and her offspring; he shall bruise your head, and you shall bruise his heel" (Genesis 3:15).

God promised that the serpent would be judged through a champion that he would send from among Eve's descendants. Though Adam and Eve had failed to resist Satan, this champion would come to judge and destroy him. The rest of the Bible tells the story of the champion God sent to defeat Satan, reverse the effects of the fall, and restore God's Kingdom in this world and in the hearts of his people. That champion is Jesus.

Jesus came to earth to break the hold that Satan has over human beings and the world God made, and he did everything that needed to be done. Though right now things are not yet the way they should be, we have God's promise that one day his kingdom will be set right again. And even now, though we still battle sin and wait for perfect peace, Jesus the champion is here, on our side and fighting for us.

What was it like for Jesus to come to earth for us? Let's look at a couple of New Testament passages, beginning with the Gospel of John.

John 1:1–14

[1] In the beginning was the Word, and the Word was with God, and the Word was God. [2] He was in the beginning with God. [3] All things were made through him, and without him was not any thing made that was made. [4] In him was life, and the life was the light of men. [5] The light shines in the darkness, and the darkness has not overcome it . . . . [9] The true light, which gives light to everyone, was coming into the world. [10] He was in the world, and the world was made through him, yet the world did not know him. [11] He came to his own, and his own people did not receive him. [12] But to all who did receive him, who believed in his name, he gave the right to become children of God . . . . [14] And the Word became flesh and dwelt among us, and we have seen his glory, glory as of the only Son from the Father, full of grace and truth.

Jesus is the Word—our champion. He is God and was with God in the beginning. He is not some abstract, impersonal force, but a distinct, individual person who speaks and acts and relates to us. His words are so powerful that when he uttered, "Let there be . . . ," the universe was formed. That eternal, personal, Creator God left his throne in heaven and entered this world to make it possible for us to be in relationship with him.

Did you get that?

Jesus left the glory of heaven to live in this broken, sinful, dark world *to be in a relationship with you*. God came down to enter your world. Not to judge you, but to be judged for you!

This is so important to understand! In the last chapter we talked about our sinfulness and our need for rescue, but take this in too: Instead of Jesus coming to condemn you for your sin, he came to take your sin on himself, to take the punishment for it as if he were the one who committed it.

Think about how hard it is for us to admit our own sin. We certainly aren't willing to take the blame for someone else's! But Jesus is different. He willingly went to the cross, as a completely innocent, sinless God-man, to take the punishment that should have been ours because of our sin. And not just for our sin, but for the sin of all his children, from Adam and Eve on. Adam and Eve deserved death for their sin, and we do too. But instead, God sent his Son Jesus to stand in our place and take our punishment, so that we could be restored to a relationship with God.

Jesus went to great lengths, both in life and in death, to bring us back to God. As you'll see in these passages from Hebrews, his time on earth is what enables him to continue to identify with us, to stick with us, to love us, and to help us every day. As you read, circle or underline any key words that help you understand that.

Hebrews 2:6–18

[6] It has been testified somewhere, "What is man, that you are mindful of him, or the son of man, that you care for him? [7] You made him for a little while lower than the angels; you have crowned him with glory and honor, [8] putting everything in subjection under his feet."

Now in putting everything in subjection to him, he left nothing outside his control. At present, we do not yet see everything in subjection to him. [9] But we see him who for a little while was made lower than the angels, namely Jesus, crowned with glory and honor because of the suffering of death, so that by the grace of God he might taste death for everyone. ¹⁰ For it was fitting that he, for whom and by whom all things exist, in bringing many sons to glory, should make the founder of their salvation perfect through suffering. ¹¹ For he who sanctifies and those who are sanctified all have one source. That is why he is not ashamed to call them brothers . . . ¹⁴ Since therefore the children share in flesh and blood, he himself likewise partook of the same things, that through death he might destroy the one who has the power of death, that is, the devil, ¹⁵ and deliver all those who through fear of death were subject to lifelong slavery. ¹⁶ For surely it is not angels that he helps, but he helps the offspring of Abraham. ¹⁷ Therefore he had to be made like his brothers in every respect, so that he might become a merciful and faithful high priest in the service of God, to make propitiation for the sins of the people. ¹⁸ For because he himself has suffered when tempted, he is able to help those who are being tempted.

Hebrews 4:14–16

¹⁴ Since then we have a great high priest who has passed through the heavens, Jesus, the Son of God, let us hold fast our confession. ¹⁵ For we do not have a high priest who is unable to sympathize with our weaknesses, but one who in every respect has been tempted as we are, yet without sin. ¹⁶ Let us then with confidence draw near to the throne of grace, that we may receive mercy and find grace to help in time of need.

The writer of Hebrews tells us that in order for Jesus to bring salvation to the world, he had to be the perfect sacrifice, and he was made perfect through suffering. But this suffering was not just what he endured on the cross. Jesus suffered throughout his entire earthly life, because in order to exchange identities with us, he had to experience everything we experience. Though he was still fully God, this did not mean that he didn't fully experience every emotion as a man. He was at the same time 100 percent man.

What this means is that Jesus knows what it is like to be misunderstood. He knows what it's like to be persecuted, mocked, and rejected. He knows what it is like to be gossiped and lied about behind his back and criticized to his face. He knows what it means to be ignored and excluded. He knows what it means to be hurt by those he loves. He knows what it means to feel sad and alone. He knows what it is like to be faced with temptation. He knows what it means to be under stress and pressure. He knows what it means to be afraid and upset. And he knows what it means to be angry.

What is amazing is that he felt every emotion we do, but without sinning! Because he experienced first-hand all that we face, he understands us completely. He knows what we go through. His suffering perfected his ability to fully identify with us. He "gets" us, and he is filled with compassion for us in our trials, temptations, and sufferings.

Because he knows us like this, we can go to him with everything. There is nothing we have to hide, nothing he can't handle, and nothing too big, too embarrassing, or too shameful to keep us from going straight to him as our Great High Priest.

In the Old Testament the high priest served as the mediator—the representative—between the people and God. Only the high priest was permitted to offer the sacrifices God required. When they were completed, he would sprinkle blood from the sacrifice onto the people as a symbolic covering for their sin. But this blood was never enough to atone for the ongoing sin of the people, so the duties of the high priest were never-ending.

Until Jesus. Jesus was a high priest like no other because he was both our mediator and our sacrifice. He fulfilled every requirement of the law with his holy, righteous, sinless life, and he then offered himself to God as the perfect sacrificial lamb on our behalf. His blood covered our sin and freed us from the curse Adam and Eve brought on the human race in the garden.

Jesus's death fulfilled God's promise to restore and redeem what was broken in the world. The cross is where we see God's most glorious display of grace, compassion, and mercy. Despite our brokenness, he declared us forgiven, perfect, and righteous, and called us to be his children. God sees us just as he sees his Son. This is what gives us our truest, most lasting and most secure identity.

On the cross, Jesus took on our identity and paid for our sin. In exchange, he gives us his perfect righteousness and we become God's children. We will talk more in the next chapter about how this great identity exchange impacts you practically, but I hope you find great comfort in knowing that our Savior was willing to face this world in order to have a personal relationship with you. He got down in the mess with you, as your compassionate friend, source of strength, and ever-present help for everything you must endure.

REFLECTION TIME

1. Why did Jesus have to become man?
2. Why is Jesus's life for you as important as his death for you?
3. How does it help to see that Jesus's suffering enables him to understand everything you go through?
4. If Jesus is personal and relational, what keeps you from talking to him like a friend?
5. How does seeing how Jesus identifies with you encourage you or change your perspective?

LAST LOOK AND JOURNALING
Read the verses below and then use the space to reflect further on the significance of Jesus identifying with you personally.

Psalm 46:1–3 | Isaiah 53:4–11 | Mark 6:1–6 | Hebrews 4:14–16

. . . .
. . . .
. . . .
. . . .
. . . .
. . . .
. . . .
. . . .
. . . .
. . . .
. . . .
. . . .
. . . .
. . . .
. . . .
. . . .
. . . .
. . . .
. . . .
. . . .

Chapter 4

"Look Full in His Wonderful Face"[2]

In the last chapter, we saw that Jesus, our champion and High Priest, willingly laid aside his glory as God to enter our world and become a man. He experienced everything we go through so that he fully understands our struggles. He lived through it all without sinning so that he could complete the work he came to earth to do: He took our sin to the cross, receiving the judgment we deserved so that God's wrath against our sin was satisfied. When Jesus proclaimed, "It is finished," we were able to be reconciled to God and become his children. There is no other friend like Jesus.

These are big theological realities. What we need to get straight is how these gospel truths impact you on a daily basis. Because Jesus was perfect, God sees anyone who trusts in Christ as Savior as perfect too. He no longer holds your sin against you—it's been paid for and forgiven. You are washed clean spiritually and you can stand before God without fear of accusation or condemnation. Everything good about him is now good about you.

This is what it means to be declared justified, or right with God. This is the doctrine of justification, a theological term not used as often as it should be, since it is a key gospel component to understanding who you are as a believer in Christ. Being united to Christ is where your infinite value comes from. This is where you get your true identity and the security that no one can take away from you.

"For our sake he [God the Father] made him [Jesus] to be sin who knew no sin, so that in him we might become the righteousness of God." (2 Corinthians 5:21)

Do you believe this?

Do you believe God loves you just as he loves his own Son?

Do you believe that even when you sin miserably, he still views you as perfect because you belong to Jesus?

If you can't say yes to these questions, don't beat yourself up for doubting. Even as Christians, we struggle (at least at times) to believe that God loves us unconditionally. And even if we really want to believe it is true, our feelings and experiences make it hard. To get a better sense as to why justification matters so much for the way you live your life, let's try to unpack this big truth practically.

Let's say you are with a group of friends and the conversation turns to gossip about a classmate. Even though you really like the girl being talked about, you go along with what the others are saying. Instead of speaking up in her defense or changing the topic, you contribute a bit to the story. Later in the day, this particular girl offers to help you with the algebra you don't understand, and you are guilt-ridden. The fact that she is being so kind while you slandered her makes it worse. You feel awful about your failure to stand up for her, so now you feel like you need to make it up to her and to God by doing something extra.

What in the world does justification have to do with this?

Everything! Here is the logic. Because you failed to be a good friend, you don't feel like you deserve her help and kindness. And the truth is, you don't! You also think that because you didn't measure up to the way God wanted you to act, you have to make up for it by working harder and doing more to be a "good" Christian. The problem with this way of thinking is that you are basing your "justification"—your security and identity in Christ—on your own performance, on how well *you* are doing, instead of who Jesus is and what he has done for you.

If Jesus has paid for your sin and declared you righteous, then even your sin does not spoil his view of you. God still views you as righteous and perfect because Jesus was righteous and perfect *for* you. In every other way you fail, he succeeded perfectly, for you. This is what is so amazing about his grace!

You may be wondering: If this is true, does our sin even matter? It seems we could just do what we want and then say we are sorry. But, yes, your sin does matter, and yes, sin is a big deal. Jesus had to die because of your sin!

What Jesus did for us does not change or lower God's requirements. He fulfilled them *for* us because no matter how "good" we try to be, we can never escape our sinful nature on our own. The fact that God views us according to Jesus's perfect record is unbelievable mercy and grace. It is when we get grace in this way—when we really see what Jesus did for us, despite our continual sin—that you want to glorify and obey him in all that you do.

So instead of feeling like you have the freedom to sin because he will forgive you anyway, you will grow to see more of your sin and to hate it. Seeing your sin is a good thing. I know that seems like an odd thing to say, but the more you see your sin, the more you know you need Jesus and the more you will live a life of repentance.

When we "get" grace, living a life of repentance should be the normal Christian life. By this I mean that, when you see your sin, you know you are free to go to God with it, repent of it, receive God's forgiveness, and ask for his strength to make things right. In his strength, you can go to those you have sinned against to confess and ask for forgiveness, knowing that even if they don't forgive you, God's view of you is unchanging.

In the case of the girl who was the subject of gossip, you don't have to try to earn God's favor back. But you might instead go to the friends who also participated in the gossip, admit that you shouldn't have said what you did, and ask them to forgive you. If the girl heard what you'd said, you will also want to seek her forgiveness instead of trying to be nice as a way of covering your sin.

Again, your standing before God does not change based on your performance. You are secure in Christ—this is the source of your true identity. This truth is what enables you, no matter what you've done, to go confidently to his throne of grace for forgiveness and help, knowing that there is no end to God's love and mercy. The God who created you and redeemed you has set his love upon you. Nothing can provide a more secure identity than this.

The problem is that we often forget this, turn away from his truth, and look to other things or people to give us significance. But this will always fail, because nothing else was meant to be our source of significance. Nothing else can make you feel secure about your worth. The identity you long for—to be accepted, included, loved, and significant—is already yours in Christ.

Jesus drives this truth home in the Gospel of Mark, when he is addressing the crowds after revealing what it means for him to be the Messiah. Think carefully about what Jesus says as you read these verses.

Mark 8:34–9:1

[34] And calling the crowd to him with his disciples, he said to them, "If anyone would come after me, let him deny himself and take up his cross and follow me. [35] For whoever would save his life will lose it, but whoever loses his life for my sake and the gospel's will save it. [36] For what does it profit a man to gain the whole world and forfeit his soul? [37] For what can a man give in return for his soul?

[38] For whoever is ashamed of me and of my words in
this adulterous and sinful generation, of him will the Son
of Man also be ashamed when he comes in the glory of
his Father with the holy angels." 9 [1] And he said to them,
"Truly, I say to you, there are some standing here who will
not taste death until they see the kingdom of God after it
has come with power."

Jesus is not trying to motivate you to follow him out of
guilt or demanding your full allegiance based on your personal
sacrifice. He is explaining what it means to truly follow him as
a disciple. To be his disciple means that you find your life in
him—you are not looking to anything or anyone else to give
you life, meaning, security, value, or any other good thing.
Another way to say this is that you find your identity by being
wrapped up in his.

On our own, we humans buy into the lies that tell us we
can find our significance and worth from the things the world
offers. We think that happiness or "life" comes through our performance, status, success, or stuff. We try to find our identity in
how well we are doing, how we look, or who we hang out with.
But Jesus tells us not to seek an identity in this way. Looking
to these things to give you worth and value will never satisfy.

Jesus wants us to know that when we try to find our
identity, worth, or value in something besides him, our very
being—who we are at our core—gets lost. For instance, let's
say you are trying to base your identity on what other people
think of you—whether you are pretty, skinny, smart, athletic,
popular, have a boyfriend or something else. It won't be long
before your "life" or joy will start to seep out as you find yourself constantly striving to achieve or maintain whatever it is
you are after. You will constantly be disappointed and most
likely depressed as you drown in self-absorption.

This is why Jesus says it will never work if you seek to gain
an identity from the things of the world. These things were

not meant to define you. They are not big enough or valuable enough to give you worth and significance. They don't have the power to give you a secure identity.

Instead, Jesus calls you to die to this way of living and find your true identity in him and in the gospel. Only he can give you a true identity, an identity that says:

- **"No matter what my peers say about me, I am deeply loved."**
- **"Even though I have messed up for the thousandth time, God calls me righteous."**
- **"Although I didn't make the team, get asked to the dance, or pass the test, my significance and worth is in Christ."**
- **"I don't have to prove or elevate myself because God accepts me as I am. His opinion is the only one that matters."**

These truths and promises run throughout God's Word. They are your sure defense. You can stand up to your anxious thoughts, insecurities, and Satan's lies when you remember the One who is your champion, your Savior, and your dearest friend. What he has done for you and given to you free you to forget yourself and to see the resurrection power of Mark 9:1 unleashed in your life.

The power that comes from Jesus's death and resurrection enables you to know:

- **Power that keeps you from looking for meaning and life from the things of this world, because Jesus is your meaning and life.**
- **Power that keeps you from trying to achieve an identity through your performance, because your identity is found in his performance for you.**
- **Power that frees you to forget yourself and focus on loving others, because you are fully and completely loved in Jesus. Now you can give yourself fully and completely to others without demanding anything in return.**

- **Power that assures you that, even though you fail in your commitment to God, you can always go to him and his grace and forgiveness are yours.**
- **Power that keeps you from being destroyed when relationships fracture or fail, because you know that Jesus will never leave you or forsake you.**
- **Power to get out of bed and keep functioning when you feel like the world is against you, because you know God is for you.**
- **Power that debunks the whispering lies and accusations of Satan.**
- **Power that leads you to share the gospel without fear to your friends.**

At the cross, Jesus won! By his resurrection power he defeated sin and Satan, and declared, "It is finished." His perfect life and sacrificial death were met by God's embrace and ensured that we too could know God's love and acceptance. By his resurrection power, we are eternally secure before God, which means that, at the cross, we won too!

When you find your true self in Jesus, you can stand when everything else is sinking around you. No matter what your weakness, struggles, sin, or brokenness, these do not define you or disqualify you for the love of Christ. It is *because* of our sin that Jesus became one with us so that we could become one with him. We can rest secure in the identity and worth he has given us.

REFLECTION TIME

1. In what ways do you see that Jesus is for you?
2. What is justification?
3. How does understanding the doctrine of justification help you find your true identity?
4. Why do you think Jesus emphasizes that finding our true identity in him is the mark of a true disciple?

5. In what ways do you still struggle to believe that your identity in him is the most secure and most real identity that you have?

LAST LOOK AND JOURNALING
Read the verses below and then use the space to write out what is true when you are in Christ.

Romans 5:1–2 | Romans 8:1–2 | Galatians 2:16–21 | Philippians 1:21

. . . .

. . . .

. . . .

. . . .

. . . .

. . . .

. . . .

. . . .

. . . .

. . . .

. . . .

. . . .

. . . .

. . . .

. . . .

. . . .

. . . .
. . . .
. . . .
. . . .
. . . .
. . . .
. . . .
. . . .
. . . .
. . . .
. . . .
. . . .
. . . .
. . . .
. . . .
. . . .
. . . .
. . . .
. . . .
. . . .
. . . .
. . . .
. . . .

Chapter 5
The Struggles We Still Face

Though you may believe that everything you have read so far in this book is true, you may still find it hard to see how Jesus's life and death are enough to satisfy you when day-to-day struggles persist. You're not alone. All of us struggle at times to believe that Jesus is enough for everything we need. We start looking to other things to fill the empty places in our hearts and give us our identity and worth.

Why is it so easy to take our eyes off Jesus and fix them on other things? Why can't life always be lived on the spiritual mountaintop where we see everything clearly, instead of constantly falling back downhill? Why is seeing who Jesus is for us so difficult?

Here is a reason you may not have expected: idolatry!

Most of us have heard this term used to talk about statues, pictures, and icons that are worshiped as representations of God in many religions. That doesn't seem to have anything to do with us. But idolatry is actually a lot more widespread than that. An idol is anyone or anything that takes God's place in your heart. Idols can set themselves up in the hearts of people of any (or no) religion, including Christians, including you. And, simply put: Whatever you worship will rule you.

If God is in his rightful place at the center of your life, his Word, his truths, and his promises will govern what you believe and how you think and act. But, as we saw in chapter 2, our sinful natures are easily deceived by Satan's lies, which seek to shift our eyes off Christ and onto something else—a pseudo-Savior or, as the Bible puts it, an idol.

Satan is always looking for ways to blind you to the truth and convince you, as he did Adam and Eve, that "life" is found in something other than God. This can happen anywhere. You may be sitting in church, listening to the sermon, when your mind starts to drift, thinking about what outfits you should wear to school that week. The next thing you know, you are looking over at a friend, wishing you had her clothes. Comparing your wardrobe to hers soon leads to you comparing yourself to everything about her. You start thinking that if you had her looks or her talent or her wardrobe or her friends, your life would be better. In a matter of minutes, you've become totally self-focused. Whatever the preacher is saying has no impact on your heart.

Do you see how subtly Satan works?

One minute you are worshipping God, and the next moment you have bowed down to a false god; that is, you've started looking for life and value from something in this world that doesn't last and will never satisfy your need. Just because you love Jesus, it doesn't automatically prevent an idol from running rampant in your heart. Over and over again, Satan lures your heart to believe idolatrous lies that promise that life can be found in external beauty, sex appeal, money, popularity, talents, accomplishments, fame, perfection or anything else. Each of these pulls you into a downward spiral of self-absorption with whatever controlling desire (idol) you are chasing—after knocking you away from your secure and true identity in Christ.

Let's go back to the example when your mind drifted at church and you wound up feeling less-than because you don't look like your friend or have her wardrobe. This kind of thinking begs you to believe that she is better than you. Instead of being thankful and confident in who God created you to be, you feel bitter and insecure because you aren't in her shoes (perhaps quite literally!). Instead of finding your worth in Jesus, you've started to believe that "life" is found in something besides him.

Only when you step back to retrace your thoughts can you see how subtly Satan twists your thoughts and takes you down dark paths, searching for something to make you feel okay or to give you significance, when all along you had it in Christ!

What I am going to say next is crucial: The fact that you struggle with idolatry and sin is actually the normal Christian life! Living life on the mountaintop, immune from temptation and confusion, is not normal—not on this earth. But as you keep listening to God, repenting and believing, trusting and following him until he takes you to your heavenly home, you will be "sanctified." That is, you will become the person you were created to be.

"Being sanctified" means that you are being made holy, being remade more and more into the image of Christ. This is an ongoing, life-long process for the believer that begins when you are justified in Christ (become a believer) and continues throughout your life, as God works to accomplish his good purpose in you. However, as you make your way through that process and live in the "in-between" of your sanctification, there will be a battle. Not only is Satan on the attack, but you'll be battling the ways of the world and your own fleshly desires too. With all three—the world, the flesh and the devil—coming at you, sometimes all at once, the fact you still struggle should not surprise you.

The following verses from Galatians and James talk about this internal tension that exists in the heart of every believer. The Holy Spirit who lives in your heart battles these spiritual enemies on your behalf. Without the indwelling Spirit, there would be no battle. On our own, we wouldn't be strong enough to fight. Temptations wouldn't exist either because, apart from God's work within us, we would always give in to the temptations Christians are called to battle.

Galatians 5:16–17

¹⁶ But I say, walk by the Spirit, and you will not gratify the desires of the flesh. ¹⁷ For the desires of the flesh are against the Spirit, and the desires of the Spirit are against the flesh, for these are opposed to each other, to keep you from doing the things you want to do.

James 4:4–8

⁴ You adulterous people! Do you not know that friendship with the world is enmity with God? Therefore whoever wishes to be a friend of the world makes himself an enemy of God. ⁵ Or do you suppose it is to no purpose that the Scripture says, "He yearns jealously over the spirit that he has made to dwell in us"? ⁶ But he gives more grace. Therefore it says, "God opposes the proud, but gives grace to the humble." ⁷ Submit yourselves therefore to God. Resist the devil, and he will flee from you. ⁸ Draw near to God, and he will draw near to you. Cleanse your hands, you sinners, and purify your hearts, you double-minded.

Both of these passages address believers—even though they are being warned as "adulterous" believers or idol-worshippers. That means all of us, since even when we are in Christ, our sin nature is still alive and active. But with God's help and the gift of the Spirit within us, we can stand up to our sin nature and fight for what God wants for us. Admittedly, because you have to fight, it may feel like life is harder for you than for your non-Christian friends. You may feel like God is ignoring you because he is not changing your situation, making things easier, answering your prayers, or taking away the struggles.

But God is not ignoring you. In the midst of ongoing struggles, sin, sadness, disappointment, failures, trials, and temptations, Jesus has promised to stay with you. He will never leave you because at the cross he committed himself to you forever. Therefore, when you are ashamed and discouraged about your latest sin and the overall fact that you are struggling, you don't have to worry that Jesus will walk away because he is angry with you or because you are angry with him for not giving you what you want. Nothing cuts you off from his loyal love. He did everything necessary to secure your relationship with him, and his unchanging, relentless pursuit of you will continue until the end.

Wow—what assurance we have, as seen in the following verses. Consider his goodness to you as you meditate on them.

Ephesians 1:11–14
[11] In him we have obtained an inheritance, having been predestined according to the purpose of him who works all things according to the counsel of his will, [12] so that we who were the first to hope in Christ might be to the praise of his glory. [13] In him you also, when you heard the word of truth, the gospel of your salvation, and believed in him, were sealed with the promised Holy Spirit, [14] who is the guarantee of our inheritance until we acquire possession of it, to the praise of his glory.

Hebrews 10:19–23
[19] Therefore, brothers, since we have confidence to enter the holy places by the blood of Jesus, [20] by the new and living way that he opened for us through the curtain, that is, through his flesh, [21] and since we have a great priest over the house of God, [22] let us draw near with a true heart in full assurance of faith, with our hearts sprinkled clean from an evil conscience and our bodies washed with pure water. [23] Let us hold fast the confession of our hope without wavering, for he who promised is faithful.

In spite of your struggle to hold on to him, Jesus never lets go of you. One of the things this means is that whatever chaos and conflict you experience, it is not a punishment for something you've done wrong. Jesus took your punishment, and it does not need to be paid a second time by you. In a similar way, positive experiences are not a result of being "blessed" for your obedience. You do not have to earn your way to stay on God's good side. Yes, you may experience the consequences of sin and the benefits of hard work, but that's a different dynamic altogether. God does not base his love for you on your performance in any way. He is neither a "policeman" out to get you, nor a "Santa Claus" handing out gifts for good behavior.

You may never know why certain things in life are part of God's plan for you. How something "bad" can possibly be used for good is often a mystery. But through it all, God is with you, making you like himself (sanctifying you) for your good and his glory. He can even take your sin and use it to accomplish the good he is doing in your life, so, believe it or not, seeing your sin is good! It shows that you are starting to see life the way God sees it, with the help of the Holy Spirit.

Do you find that hard to believe? Would you rather sweep your sin under the rug and pretend it's not there? Do you even allow yourself to acknowledge the sinful motives, desires, and idols inside you?

What's going on inside is easy to overlook, to hide even from ourselves, and to justify to others. For instance that is what's happening when you act impatient and then justify it by saying that's just how God made you. You might minimize your rudeness by saying that your personality just likes to say it how it is. You may not be in the habit of confessing and repenting of your sin because you don't realize how deep and frequent your sin is! And let's face it, when you are comparing yourself to other sinful people like yourself, the temptation is to excuse and minimize the ugly stuff you know is buried deep down inside you because you fear what others would think, forgetting that they have their own set of struggles and sins. If you recall the survey results in the beginning of the book, we all do. We just tend to forget, so we wear a mask portraying to the world that we have it all together.

The wonderful part about seeing and admitting your sin is that it shows you why you need Jesus as your Savior. This leads to greater dependence on the One who paid for your sin and made you God's well-loved daughter. Learning to identify and repent of the idols that crop up in your life will lead you to the place of worship and gratitude as you see who he has made you to be. And more and more, you will want to become like him, not the people around you.

Facing your idols happens as you learn to uncover the lies you believe and replace them with God's truth. This is why your one true defense is praying and studying God's Word, knowing who Jesus is for you, and going to him, even—especially!—when you struggle with sin. You can ask God to help you do this and to move your heart to peace and rest in him.

I hope that the knowledge that in Christ you are deeply loved, accepted, and perfect is beginning to take root inside you. Looking to anything or anyone else for this will always leave you empty. Only in Jesus will you find your true identity, value, and security. He is the only One who can make you whole and give you true "life."

Part II of this book will apply the gospel truths and promises of these past chapters to the very practical struggles facing girls at your time of life. As you read, I hope you will see how knowing your identity in Christ and what he's done for you is the foundation to a life of freedom, contentment, and joy, no matter what you are up against.

REFLECTION TIME

1. What are some of the idols you turn to as you seek other people's approval or a sense of your own worth?
2. Why is seeing these idols for what they are a good thing?

3. As you identify some of these idols, list some truths about who you are in Christ that combat the lies.
4. What hope do you find, despite the fact you will still struggle?
5. What is the true identity Christ gives you?
6. How can these truths keep your heart secure?

LAST LOOK AND JOURNALING
Read the verses below and then write out a prayer asking God to help you to seek true life in him, not in chasing after false gods.

Exodus 20:3 | Matthew 6:19–21 | Romans 1:21–25 | Colossians 2:6–10

· ·

· ·

· ·

· ·

· ·

· ·

· ·

· ·

· ·

· ·

· ·

· ·

· ·

· ·
· ·
· ·
· ·
· ·
· ·
· ·
· ·
· ·
· ·
· ·
· ·
· ·
· ·
· ·
· ·
· ·
· ·
· ·
· ·
· ·

Part II:

* * * * * * * * *

Facing False Identities

In Part I, we looked at what Jesus has done for you, and how that lays the foundation for seeing yourself rightly, the way God sees you. When you start to understand that Jesus's perfect life and death makes you forgiven and righteous in God's sight, you will stand more secure. You will find greater peace, knowing that his love for you is what gives you your significance and infinite worth. Now, when you feel crushed under the weight of your sin, others' opinions, or the brokenness of the world, you know that you can and must go back to the gospel. Specifically, you must remember what it means to be justified—that when the God of the universe set his love on you, he did everything necessary to make you right with him. Because of Jesus's death on your behalf, God calls you his child and looks at you the way he looks at his own Son! Let that sink into your soul!

In Part II, you are going to practice applying the truths we've talked about. You will *need* practice because, as we saw in the last chapter, you will struggle and often fail, even as a Christian. But when you remember who God is for you and how you can apply that promise to all of life, you can experience security and freedom as a deeply loved and for-given sinner.

The stories in this section are fictional, but based on strug-gles common to teen girls. After each story, a set of questions will help you analyze what was going on, what lies were being believed by the main character, and what truths are needed to replace the lies. Spend some time thinking about the answers on your own, and then read the summary that follows to give you more insight and understanding.

Don't be discouraged if reading the summary makes you feel as if you didn't come up with the right answers to the ques-tions. Understanding how to see ourselves from God's point of view takes time—and in a sense, we're never done. As long as we live, Satan will try to lure us away from the truth of God's Word. But God will help you to know more of his love so that you can rest more securely in him. So don't give up! Practicing will help prepare you for whatever might come your way.

Story 1
Comparisons

If Kennedy added up the amount of time she spends on social media each day, it would likely be about three hours. Each morning, before even getting out of bed, she scrolls through her sites to see what was posted while she was sleeping. The buzz alerting her to new posts and stories starts at breakfast and continues throughout the day and into the night. Because she is constantly checking—while getting dressed, between classes, after school, with her friends, at the gym, during dinner—she is distracted, no matter where she is, what she is doing, or who she is with.

In Kennedy's mind, this behavior is completely normal. Everyone else does the same thing, and if she wants to keep up with everything going on around her, she must too. If she weren't connected, she would feel like she was missing out.

Still, at the same time, every picture that's posted causes her to cringe inside. She can't help but feel rejected, even by good friends, when she sees things she hasn't been invited to and parties she has missed.

She wonders, why wouldn't she be included? Don't they like her? Did she do something wrong? Why was so-and-so included and not her?

These are the thoughts running through her mind, but she would never actually ask the other girls about it or let them know they've hurt her. She feels like she has nowhere to go with her fears, so feelings of being "less-than" start to consume her.

Kennedy's worries about not measuring up are intensified by the fact that everybody else always looks perfect and has it all together. Perfect hair, perfect bodies, perfect outfits, perfect boyfriends, and perfect vacations make it impossible to keep up. She will never be as pretty, as smart, as athletic, or as popular as her friends. Nor does her family have the money to afford all the designer stuff everyone else has. How can she even begin to compete?

Because Kennedy is constantly comparing herself to others, she can't walk down the hall at school without scanning every girl she passes. She would never admit to being a jealous person, so she doesn't see her discontent as envy. But maybe that's what it is. Another thing Kennedy doesn't see is how her struggles are damaging her relationships with her friends. All she can see is that she is one big hopeless failure.

Now it's your turn to determine where Kennedy has stopped believing the gospel.

If the gospel worked its way into her heart, how would it change where she is seeking to find her identity?

REFLECTION TIME
1. What are the lies Kennedy believes to be true?
2. What has led her to live in a false reality?
3. What are the truths she needs to remember?
4. How would the promises and truths of the gospel keep her from feeling like she doesn't measure up?
5. How do you relate to Kennedy?
6. If you believed your answer to #4, how would it help you to avoid comparing yourself to others?

TRUTH TIME
Kennedy does not see how her social media use contributes to her feelings of failure and worthlessness. But just as a recovered alcoholic would be wise to avoid hanging out in

a bar, Kennedy would benefit from a break from the constant images of social media. However, deleting her social media accounts would not provide the ultimate solution because it does not address the underlying problem.

This is because the real problem is in her heart, the sin within. Even if Kennedy avoided all social media, she would still walk the halls at school, attend social events, read magazines, and have conversations with friends that would spark insecurity, envy, and jealousy. (Having said that, I would add that if comparing yourself to others is a real struggle for you, you might be wise to temporarily delete or limit your access to social media. Don't go back to it until you can look at it without feeling the anxiety Kennedy experienced.)

Kennedy believed that she could never match up to her peers because they seemed better than her in every way. It didn't matter how pretty, smart, talented, athletic, or wonderful she was; she only saw herself as a failure in comparison to those around her. Her perceived "truth" had replaced what God said about her and blinded her to his truths.

Kennedy's "truth" bases her value, identity, and worth on how she sees herself—which she assumes is how others must view her too. When she says that she is not as pretty or as thin as her friends, she concludes that she is not good enough. When she sees posts of friends at a party without her, she believes she is unacceptable, unworthy to be associated with them. When she falsely sees others as perfect, she assumes that their lives are great, which makes her feel worse about hers. As these negative thoughts pile up, Kennedy's once-secure identity has tanked; she sees herself as a nobody.

But God presents a very different picture. God's Word declares Kennedy to be a child of God, holy and blameless before him (Ephesians 1:4). God's truth declares her righteous (Romans 5:9), deeply loved (Romans 8:39), and fearfully and wonderfully made (Psalm 139:14).

How different Kennedy would feel if she believed these words instead of, like Eve, listening to lies from the pit of hell! If she trusted God as the reigning authority in her life, she would be able to rejoice in the fact that her Creator had formed her to be exactly as she is. Like all of humanity, she is stamped "made in his image" and considered of infinite value. This is where her true worth comes from, not from where she ranks among her friends.

On top of that, God set his special love upon her, sending his Son to the cross on her behalf, so she could be clothed in his holy, righteous perfection. This means that when God looks at her, he sees her as perfect!

Wow! Just what Kennedy longs to be! And, just like Eve, she has failed to see that she is chasing after what she already has.

Kennedy listens to the wrong voices. She believes that what she sees is what's true, not what God declares to be true. When she starts down that road, Kennedy must remember again whose opinion is the only one that matters; whose voice is the final authority offering undeniable truth.

Sometimes this is hard to believe because what God says in his Word doesn't feel as real as what you "see." If this is where you are right now, I encourage you to open your Bible to the passages listed. Ask God to help you believe what he's promised you. May his truths about who you are in him be your resting place!

LAST LOOK AND JOURNALING

Insert your name in the verses below and ask God to help you believe that they are true.

Jeremiah 1:5 | Song of Solomon 4:7 | Ephesians 2:10

· ·

· ·

· ·

· ·

· ·

· ·

· ·

· ·

· ·

· ·

· ·

· ·

· ·

· ·

· ·

· ·

· ·

· ·

. . . .
. . . .
. . . .
. . . .
. . . .
. . . .
. . . .
. . . .
. . . .
. . . .
. . . .
. . . .
. . . .
. . . .
. . . .
. . . .
. . . .
. . . .
. . . .
. . . .
. . . .
. . . .
. . . .
. . . .

Story 2
Body Image

Elena has always loved to dance. She feels so free on the stage, even in front of a crowd. Growing up, her favorite time of the year was recital time, but just going to dance classes was a highlight of her week.

As a younger girl, she looked up to the high school drill team girls who helped teach the dance classes. She wanted to be just like them and couldn't wait to be old enough to perform on the school team wearing their uniform. Finally, the time came to try out, and with her dance experience Elena made the team with ease. By her sophomore year, she had even advanced to an officer position.

During this same time, however, Elena was going through puberty. Her once-thin frame had morphed into a body she no longer recognized. Now she felt large compared to the other girls, and she *was* larger than she once had been. For the first time, Elena felt insecure while performing.

Every Friday night when she got dressed in her uniform, she couldn't help but look at the other girls, wishing her legs were as thin as theirs. She hated having to stand next to them. She just knew that everybody in the stadium must be thinking she didn't belong with all the other beauties.

As these thoughts began to dominate her, Elena became more self-focused and less free. It wasn't just about her legs anymore; now she obsessed over her disproportionately small chest, along with every blemish and the whiteness (or lack thereof) of her teeth. Nothing was quite right and she hated it.

Elena started spending more money on beauty products that promised instant results and more time in front of the mirror getting ready. But she was never satisfied. The steady stream of self-degrading commentary was always running through her head. She had become so used to it that she didn't even realize how it was controlling her. She was consumed by thoughts like, *Why did God make me like this?* and *If only I looked like so-and-so, life would be great.*

In the midst of this self-absorption, Elena didn't realize that she had begun to isolate herself from her friends by routinely backing out of plans they had together. She was so ensnared by her idol of personal perfection that she could no longer think past herself to care about other people, as she once had. She could no longer find joy in the gift of dance that God had given her. She couldn't even enjoy life as a high school sophomore.

Now it is your turn to detect where Elena has stopped believing the gospel and based her identity on lies.

REFLECTION TIME

1. What are the lies consuming Elena?
2. Why has she bought into these lies?
3. What truths does she need to remember about who Jesus is for her?
4. How would this help her to accept her body?
5. How do you relate to Elena?
6. If you believed your answer to #4, how would it help you to be thankful for the way God made you, instead of wishing you could change something about yourself?

TRUTH TIME

What has happened to Elena is very similar to Kennedy's struggle with comparison. When Elena started comparing her body to those of her teammates, she turned in on herself and began obsessing about her external appearance. Social media was not the problem this time; it was being around other dancers who (Elena thought) looked better in their uniforms. But both Kennedy and Elena had tied their identity to something other than God.

Elena could quit the team and stop dancing, but would that eliminate her body image issues?

No, of course not. Her distorted thinking about her body is coming from inside, from her own heart. She, too, has fallen for the lie that the serpent told Eve, accusing God of withholding something from her. It is a lie that questions God's love and causes Elena to think, "If God really loved me, why didn't he make me different?"

Have you ever felt this way? Do you ever obsessively wish that something about you could be changed?

For Elena—and perhaps for you—negative self-talk must be replaced by the truth of God's Word. His truth alone has the power to change hearts. And change from the inside out is what is needed for Elena to see what God calls beautiful. God's definition is completely different from what the world says: "For the LORD sees not as man sees: man looks on the outward appearance, but the LORD looks on the heart" (1 Samuel 16:7b).

It is the inside—the heart, the soul, and the mind—that is the core of who we are. How we think, what we believe, who or what we worship are what matter, not that our thighs may be too large and our left side doesn't photograph well! Our inside is what actually bears God's image.

When God looked at man and called him "good," it was God's own perfect image he saw reflected, as displayed in the holiness, compassion, kindness, humility, meekness, patience, and love human beings had before the fall. But in Elena's self-centered struggles, her inner beauty has become lost.

What if Elena lived instead according to her true identity of having been fearfully and wonderfully made in his image? What if she held onto his promise that, in Christ, she was God's workmanship, set apart for good works that had already been prepared for her? What if she really understood that God's great and personal love for her was what led him to send his Son to die for her?

When Elena's trust in God's promise helps her take her eyes off herself, she can focus instead on the people he has placed in her path. She can find her God-given purpose by seeking to love others well. Her self-absorption and her self-loathing would start to fade. By reflecting Jesus from the inside out, her true beauty would shine and the external flaws she once fixated on would no longer dominate her thoughts.

What freedom there is when you realize that the King of all things and the masterpiece-maker declares that you, his redeemed daughter, are "altogether beautiful . . . there is no flaw in you" (Song of Solomon 4:7)! May this truth be your source of hope and joy!

LAST LOOK AND JOURNALING
Using the following verses as a springboard, write a prayer praising God for the way he created you.

Genesis 1:26 | Psalm 139:14 | Ephesians 4:24

. . . .

. . . .

. . . .

. . . .

. . . .

. . . .

. . . .

. . . .

. . . .

. . . .
. . . .
. . . .
. . . .
. . . .
. . . .
. . . .
. . . .
. . . .
. . . .
. . . .
. . . .
. . . .
. . . .
. . . .
. . . .
. . . .
. . . .
. . . .
. . . .
. . . .
. . . .

Yvette has always felt like a giant next to all her super-skinny, petite, and perfect friends. When they post pictures, she cringes in fear that everyone else will see her as she sees herself—the "fat" one in the group. Her gorgeous mane of hair and big bright eyes seem like nothing to her. All she sees is her round face, broad shoulders, and missing six-pack. When her mom tells her it's what's inside that truly makes one beautiful, it doesn't help. Looking "hot" and wearing a certain dress size are what make someone beautiful in Yvette's world.

Yvette has tried various diets in the past, but after a few days or maybe a week of no carbs, no sugar, or only shakes, her body revolts and any weight lost comes back with a vengeance. This time, though, she is determined to become as thin, if not thinner, than her friends.

Armed with her weight loss app for logging all foods and strictly counting calories, Yvette begins to see results. Based on such early success, she decides that if she restricts her food intake to an even greater degree, she will lose weight even faster. So she does and, with each pound dropped, her determination grows even stronger.

Though she felt better and believed she looked better, it wasn't until other people began to compliment her that she felt really good about herself. The feeling she got when people told her how great she looked fed her desire to be even thinner.

Yvette's calorie consumption kept decreasing and the foods she ate were limited to about ten things. She stopped menstruating and her energy level dropped, but when her parents tried to talk to her about their concerns, she was defensive and denied there was a problem.

She loved being able to wear anything and look good in it. She enjoyed being noticed for the first time by cute boys. But her friends grew more and more concerned as Yvette began skipping out on any social plans that included food. Soon she started to withdraw altogether. It seemed that their once healthy and vibrant friend had faded away along with the lost pounds. When one of them finally gained the courage to talk to her about it, Yvette dismissed the concern, just as she had with her parents.

Yvette could not see how depleted her body was of needed nutrients. She couldn't gauge the toll it took on her internal organs. Neither could Yvette see how her obsession with food and her appearance had blinded her to what was happening in her heart. As ridiculous as it may sound, food had become her god. Her every thought and action was tied to what she would eat and how she looked. She had no understanding of the physical help and spiritual awakening she so desperately needed.

Now it is your turn to detect where Yvette has stopped believing the gospel and is basing her identity on lies.

REFLECTION TIME

1. What is the root that led Yvette down the path to an eating disorder?
2. What makes the root cause (or idolatry) a deeper problem than the eating disorder?
3. How might the eating disorder issues change if the idols ruling Yvette's heart were addressed first and didn't have such a hold on her?
4. What makes Jesus's love greater than what Yvette seeks from other people?

5. What other truths about who Jesus is would help Yvette regain perspective?
6. In what ways do you identify with Yvette? How do you need to see Jesus as greater in your life?

TRUTH TIME

Although Yvette would never admit it, she is engulfed in a full-fledged eating disorder. Eating disorders and disordered eating come in various forms and can look completely different in different individuals. One of the most challenging aspects of recovering, apart from acknowledging the need for help, is that food is not the real issue behind an eating disorder. It is as much a spiritual battle and heart problem as a mental and physical challenge.

In Yvette's case, she cannot see the long-term damage to her overall health. Even the fact that she has become too skinny does not register with her. While she may be somewhat aware of the problem, she isn't willing to admit it because how she looks and feels is more important to her. Something other than God is ruling her heart, and the problem of the eating disorder can only be properly addressed after that idol is faced.

Yvette's harmful eating patterns intensified over time, but the idols ruling her heart were present long before dieting morphed into an eating disorder. From the outside, it may look as if her food restrictions are the sole problem. In actuality, her thoughts had been taken captive before she'd lost a single pound.

From the start, Yvette was discontent with her appearance, especially in comparison to her friends. We have looked at these issues in the first two stories, but now they are manifesting themselves in a different way. At the root of Yvette's eating disorder is her false thinking that "life" or her ultimate happiness will be found in her appearance and the acceptance it will bring. She believes that if she looks a certain way, she will feel more confident, be more popular, find a boyfriend, and get more attention. She is living as if controlling her food will control how others view her, resulting in the glory and status she longs for. It's a false source of identity.

Don't we all want to be great? I mean, can't you identify with Yvette's desires even if an eating disorder isn't your issue? If we are honest, we all want recognition, validation, and praise to some degree. But Yvette has made a good thing an ultimate thing—something she believes she cannot live without.

What are the lies Yvette believes that need to be replaced with truth? What is she forgetting—and perhaps you are too?

For starters, Yvette believes that her worth is based on something other than Christ. Life will be great if she looks great—or so she thinks. Not only that, but if she looks better than her friends do, she will feel better about herself. Perhaps others will even be jealous of her! The attention she would receive will make her feel important and more significant.

Can you see how these idolatrous thoughts can perpetuate an eating disorder? In order to achieve and maintain what rules her, Yvette must constantly strive to be thinner. One pound in the wrong direction would threaten to undo what she has worked so hard for, so there is no end to the obsession with how she looks and how she is viewed.

The oppression of living under that burden will not provide her with the happiness and life she thinks it will. In fact, the longer she bows down to these false gods, the more she will sink into herself and drift further away from God's life-giving truths.

Yvette needs to know God's love for her—experientially. She may say, "I know God loves me," but she doesn't really know the greatness of his love until she realizes that it is shown in the greatness of his sacrifice. You can say that honey is sweet, but until you taste it, you don't truly know. Because if she did, wouldn't knowing how much God loves her carry more weight than how others view her?

How sweet is the love of Jesus, once you taste and see that it is the only thing that can satisfy the deepest longings of your heart! His acceptance is unconditional and his love unrelenting. Embracing these truths is what Yvette—and all of us—need to do, whatever our false gods are.

LAST LOOK AND JOURNALING

Read the following verses and then write down what the love of Jesus means for you personally.

Romans 5:8 | Ephesians 2:4–5 | 1 John 4:9–10

Kim is grounded again from weeknight activities. This time it's because of the "B" she got on her AP world history test. Her parents worry that clubs and sports are taking precedence over her studies. What they don't realize is that Kim's failure to get an "A" was upsetting enough to her on its own—she doesn't need their extra pressure to bring up her grade. But the truth is, everything feels like a battle with her parents. Last week they wouldn't allow her to go to a friend's party because she'd missed curfew the weekend before. Even though she'd called to say that she unexpectedly had to drop off a friend, no excuses are acceptable.

Out of all Kim's friends, she is the one who is the rule follower. Why can't her parents see how good they have it with a daughter like her? Why do they have to be so strict and uncompromising? Why do they worry so much? Why can't they be like other people's parents?

Kim is sick of trying to live by their rules and meet their expectations. She doesn't like being around their constant nagging. She doesn't need it, given the pressure she already feels internally. On her own, Kim has taken her parents' pressure and taken it even further. She craves their approval and wants their praise, and this desire to know that she is acceptable has created in her an insatiable drive to be the best. She has set herself the goal of being the absolute best at everything she does, so that no one will have a legitimate reason to criticize her.

But just as she falls short of her parents' expectations, Kim has trouble meeting her own uncompromising standards. A single flaw, missed opportunity, or unmet expectation floods her with the feeling of failure. Whether she is berating herself for less-than-perfect grades, forgetting to do something, or saying something foolish, she is her own worst critic. In her mind, she should have done better. The impossible standard of perfection keeps pushing Kim to try harder.

If you looked at her activities and grades, you would never suspect that Kim could possibly feel this way. From the looks of it, she is Miss Everything. But nothing—the grades, the activities, the awards—is ever enough. She is always one step below where she thinks she should be. And unbeknownst to everyone who tells her that she is amazing, Kim is on the brink of a breakdown.

Now it is your turn to detect where Kim has lost sight of the gospel. How would the gospel's promises change where she is seeking to find her identity?

REFLECTION TIME

1. Where is Kim seeking to find her worth?
2. Why does she think she must meet these self-imposed standards?
3. What happens when she doesn't meet those standards?
4. What is Kim failing to believe about God?
5. What makes you feel like a failure?
6. When you feel this way, on what are you basing your identity and worth?

TRUTH TIME

It is easy to imagine Kim as the type of student that teachers single out as a role model, or the one her peers try to imitate. Her accomplishments, her drive, and her hard work cause her to shine. You probably know someone a lot like Kim. Or maybe you *are* Kim.

Teenagers are under a lot of pressure to build the best resume by taking advanced level classes, serving in leadership positions, and participating in as many extra-curricular clubs and activities as possible. There is little room to be average. It's no longer good enough to just be cute, to just be on the soccer team, or to make As and Bs. No: Only being drop-dead gorgeous, the star player, and class valedictorian will do. So you live under the enormous weight of trying to be the person you think you must be in order to feel good about yourself, please your parents, and lead others to admire you.

When this happens, you mistakenly believe, like Kim, that your worth is measured by your accomplishments. But if you believe that your identity is tied to your performance, as you see with Kim, then there is no rest for the weary—*ever*—because there is always something more to do. You look around and see others performing better, so you put yourself in competition with them. But with the standard constantly changing, there is never a time when there isn't more work to do.

Another problem for Kim is the crushing blow she feels internally any time she makes a mistake. Anything less than perfect is unsatisfactory, not only because of pressure from her parents but also because of pressure she places on herself. She feels as if she has to overcompensate for any failure, doing whatever is necessary to make up for her flaws.

When parents add an extra level of pressure, it is natural to want to please them. It is important, though, to realize that they too are sinners, prone to seek an identity in false ways. Often, parents mistakenly look to their children's success as the basis of their own worth. While it can be challenging to respectfully broach this topic with your parents (and, unfortunately, it may fall on deaf ears), expressing how you are being affected by the weight of their expectations is important. How they respond is outside your control, but there is One—your heavenly Father—who declares his children to be enough. Not because of how you perform, but because of what Jesus did for you.

A light bulb may be going off in your head as you recall discussing justification in Part I of this book. If you remember, *justification* is "to be made right." It is the one-time act when Jesus exchanged his perfect, righteous life with our sin, so that we are declared justified. For those who trust in Christ for their salvation, absolutely everything needed for them to be right with God has already been accomplished by Jesus's death on the cross.

When Kim tells herself that she must perfectly perform and achieve, she is forgetting and negating the work that Christ has already declared "finished." She is acting as if what he did was not enough. She is placing more value in her own performance than the perfect standard Christ has already attained for her.

Kim is living, as we often do, as if she must save herself. In her constant quest to achieve perfection, she is acting as if she can or must attain a certain level of righteousness on her own in order to be worthy. But justification is what we need, because it is through justification that we are given Christ's righteousness, and only through *his* righteousness that we are saved. Kim needs to go back to justification as the foundational truth for her life.

Kim needs to rest in Jesus's work for her as the source of her identity and worth, instead of trying to justify herself through her own efforts. Whether or not she achieves certain goals, is honored for her accomplishments, or perfectly excels at anything, they are not what give her value. Living as if they can will ensnare her in idolatry. She is perfect already because Jesus was perfect for her! This is why theology matters. The truth of justification is what needs to work its way into her heart so that she is no longer enslaved to working out her own salvation.

LAST LOOK AND JOURNALING

Meditate on the passage below and then write out a prayer, asking God to help you see his finished work as all you need to be enough.

2 Peter 1:3–11

. . . .

. . . .

. . . .

. . . .

. . . .

. . . .

. . . .

. . . .

. . . .

. . . .

. . . .

. . . .

. . . .

. . . .

. . . .

. . . .

. . . .

. . . .

. . . .
. . . .
. . . .
. . . .
. . . .
. . . .
. . . .
. . . .
. . . .
. . . .
. . . .
. . . .
. . . .
. . . .
. . . .
. . . .
. . . .
. . . .
. . . .
. . . .
. . . .
. . . .
. . . .

"**C**ute bag!" "Fun top!" "That dress is awesome!" "Oh my gosh—you have another new pair of (insert latest designer)!"

Such are the daily compliments that feed Ava's ego as she walks down the hall at school. She has gone all year without wearing the exact same outfit. It has become her claim to fame and a streak she has no intention of breaking.

Money isn't an issue for Ava's family, so buying whatever she wants at any high-end store in town is no big deal. Along with shopping, her usual weekend line-up consists of eating out and attending concerts and sporting events. That is, unless her family goes to their lake house for the weekend, as they often do, or on a long weekend getaway to more exotic destinations.

Ava takes it for granted that she can do a lot of things others cannot, but she is very much aware of the attention that comes with posting pictures of it all. With such an extravagant lifestyle, she is almost always the center of attention, the one everyone wants to be close with. That kind of adoration has boosted Ava's feeling of self-importance and her aura of being better than everyone around her. But it has also made her compulsive about making sure that she is always the best dressed and seen at every event.

Ava's friends wish they had what she has and envy her life. For Piper in particular, a new desire is sparked in her each time she sees Ava with a new item. Piper usually doesn't wear earrings, but when she saw the pair Ava bought, she longed for a pair for herself. But for Piper to purchase the earrings means saving up her hard-earned babysitting money first.

Attaching herself to Ava makes Piper feel important. But there is a cost involved: The more time she spends with Ava, the more aware Piper is of what she doesn't have. Jealousy and discontent consume her.

Believe it or not, dissatisfaction is running through Ava too. She can get everything she wants, but she still feels empty and pressured inside and doesn't know why. So she continues to distract herself with more stuff and to search for the high that comes with the latest wave of compliments.

Now it is your turn to detect where Ava and Piper have stopped believing the gospel. If the gospel really penetrated their hearts, how would it change where they are seeking to find their identity?

REFLECTION TIME

1. What is Ava turning to for her worth?
2. What is Piper looking to for her value?
3. How are their hearts the same, even though they are in different positions?
4. Why do you think it might be harder for Ava to see that she struggles with materialism?
5. As they base their identities on what they have or don't have, what lies are Ava and Piper believing?
6. What makes the false god of materialism easy for you to justify or ignore?

TRUTH TIME

The labels. The attention. The feeling of superiority—secretly, Ava loves it all. She doesn't see the sin mingled in with it or how that sin is controlling her and leading to emptiness. She could easily point out that there is nothing wrong with liking nice things, and that's true. And, since her family can afford them, what is the problem?

The problem is that Ava does more than *like* nice things. She is living as if her worth comes from her possessions and activities. They have become her god—the thing she relies on for life and for her own value and security. She feels more important and valuable than others because of what she has and what she gets to do. So, on top of the idolatry, there is pride.

Perhaps the only way for Ava to see how materialism consumes her is to consider how she would feel if it all were taken away. Would she still be okay? Would she be able to let it go?

A good test for Ava, and for us, to help evaluate whether something is an idol is the clenched fist/open hand analogy.[3] If you are holding on to something so tightly that you are unwilling to let it go, then it is an idol. That person, thing, or desire is what you are functionally worshipping; it's what is ruling you. But if you are able to hold it loosely in an open hand, content with or without the person, thing, or desire, it likely does not have an idolatrous hold on your life. Another way to assess whether or not something is a ruling idol in your life is to consider your emotions. If that something were taken from you, how would you feel? How you respond is telling.

Ava is ruled by materialism. She falsely believes that what she has and does makes her more important than others. The wardrobe, the excitement, the extras of life, are what she thinks will give her life value and meaning. Yet she is dissatisfied and constantly searching for more things, more attention, and more praise. Only Christ can give her infinite worth and a secure identity.

This is true for Piper too. Piper doesn't have what Ava does, but she covets it, thinking that "if only" she had more, she would be happier and seen as more important. She attaches herself to Ava to make herself feel more worthy. Piper does not see how she, too, is being ruled by materialism.

Both girls are looking to something other than Jesus for their identity. Both believe that the temporary pleasures and riches of the world are more valuable than the riches a life in

Christ brings. They keep trying to make more of themselves through pursuing a certain lifestyle, yet both are empty.

In contrast, Paul had this to say about contentment in Philippians 4:13: ". . . for I have learned in whatever situation I am to be content. I know how to be brought low, and I know how to abound. In any and every circumstance, I have learned the secret of facing plenty and hunger, abundance and need. I can do all things through him who strengthens me."

Whether you identify more with Ava or with Piper, the secret to contentment will never be found in more stuff or greater prestige. It's only found when you are anchored to the One who is more valuable than silver and gold, the One who crowns you with his glory. When you find your fulfillment in him, you can be okay with whatever your circumstance.

LAST LOOK AND JOURNALING
Take an honest look at your heart to see where you find yourself in these passages. Use the space below to write a prayer of confession. Then ask God to help you see how truly rich you are when you know and trust him.

Matthew 19:23–24 | 1 Timothy 6:9–10 | James 2:2–5

....
....
....
....
....
....
....
....
....
....
....
....
....
....
....
....
....
....
....
....
....
....

. . . .
. . . .
. . . .
. . . .
. . . .
. . . .
. . . .
. . . .
. . . .
. . . .
. . . .
. . . .
. . . .
. . . .
. . . .
. . . .
. . . .
. . . .
. . . .
. . . .
. . . .
. . . .

Story 6
Friends

Ashlyn hung out with a "good" group of kids. She felt for-tunate that halfway through her junior year she was still surrounded by so many girls and guys who didn't party. Yet she sensed something lacking in her friendships. No one else in the group seemed to feel the way she did. Being known for their good behavior and strong moral convictions seemed like a great witness to others and was something they all took pride in, but what Ashlyn experienced within the group left her empty.

One Friday night, the group went to a restaurant to cele-brate a girl's birthday. Ashlyn sat in the middle of the table with conversations on every side of her, yet she felt incredibly alone.

She wondered, would they even notice if I weren't here? Do they care about me as an individual or do they only care about being part of this group with a good reputation? Or was post-ing pictures of the party the only thing anyone cared about?

These nagging feelings had been eating at Ashlyn for months. She had suppressed them, afraid that no one would understand how she could feel this way. It did seem strange to be surrounded by such a moral group of friends and yet feel like there was so much missing. It all seemed so impersonal. It seemed like no one really knew how to care about each other.

After the birthday dinner, all the girls spent the night together, but Ashlyn just wanted to go home. She made up an excuse as to why she couldn't stay, got in her car, and called her mom in tears as she drove home.

As Ashlyn talked to her mom, she kept saying how ready she was to get away and go to college. Ashlyn's mom didn't want her to wish away her remaining time in high school or unnecessarily separate herself from the group, but Ashlyn didn't know how she could keep putting up with the self-absorption of everyone around her. She longed for a real, caring friend; a friend she could share honestly with, a friend who really cared about her.

Without a friend like that in the group, Ashlyn felt hopeless that anything would change. And, just as her mom anticipated, Ashlyn began to distance herself from the group, not seeing that she too had become totally self-absorbed.

Now it is your turn to detect where Ashlyn has stopped believing the gospel and is basing her identity on lies.

REFLECTION TIME

1. Identify and list the problem areas in this story.
2. In what ways can "goodness" and morality be as destructive as outright rebellion?
3. What truths about Christ does Ashlyn need to remember?
4. How would truth keep her from withdrawing into herself, but motivate her instead to reach out to love others?
5. What friend issues have you experienced that have caused you pain, loneliness, and/or self-pity?
6. If you believed your answer to #4, how would it help you be a more compassionate, true friend, even when others don't treat you that way?

TRUTH TIME

It may seem a little trickier to discern how gospel truth needs to penetrate Ashlyn's heart, since it is her friends who appear to be the problem. But, while they are not acting as true friends should, our task here is to understand what's going on in Ashlyn's heart.

Let's assume that Ashlyn is exactly right in what she sees about her friends' self-absorption. They care more about being included in the group than about loving and investing in individual friends. It's no wonder she felt hurt. However, we must admit that it's unlikely that they were deliberately dismissing her because they didn't like her or that they wouldn't notice or care if she wasn't there. They were probably just so preoccupied with themselves that they didn't realize how Ashlyn could've felt mistreated and ignored. So we will assume that their behavior was not personal toward Ashlyn, even though it's understandable that she took it that way.

The "holy huddle" reputation these kids have acquired came about because they don't drink or engage in other overtly sinful behavior. But what they don't see is how their "goodness" not only fuels their thinking that they are better than others, but blinds them to their own sin. Sins such as pride, elevating ourselves as better, and judging others are easily hidden because they are internal, private sins. This is likely why Ashlyn felt like no one understood what she felt. As Christians, we must be honest to see that we still succumb to sin.

In processing the situation as Ashlyn did, without having an honest conversation with any of her friends, she made assumptions about their intentions and built up resentment toward people she had a long history with. While Ashlyn's gut reaction may have been spot on, her mom could have encouraged Ashlyn to prayerfully and gently talk to a couple of the girls privately about her feelings. As Proverbs 17:17 tells us, "A friend loves at all times, and a brother is born for adversity," so a conversation like this might help bring this group closer together in more authentic and fulfilling friendships.

If, for whatever reason, Ashlyn couldn't confront them (or perhaps she tried and was not understood), then what should she do? What did Ashlyn need most? The same thing we all need most, even if we have strong friendships. Ultimately, there is only One who will ever be the perfect friend; the One whose love was so great that he laid down his life for you. His name is Jesus.

As we saw in Part I, Jesus is relational and therefore wants you to relate to him as a friend. You can and should confide in him all that you are feeling and experiencing. His love is so great that nothing is too small or insignificant to bring to him.

When we bring Jesus our relational hurts and see that he is the only perfect friend, we are then confronted with the fact that we aren't always the perfect friend either. Though we don't know if or how Ashlyn had mistreated her friends, we do know that her resentment caused her to isolate herself from them. But if she was reminded that we are all broken sinners who live for ourselves and aren't always very good friends, wouldn't that have helped her to be more compassionate?

Perhaps remembering this truth would have enabled her to give grace and understanding to friends who, like her, wanted to feel included and important. Perhaps seeing this truth would have helped her to move toward them in love as a good friend even when she did not feel supported. Perhaps this truth would have encouraged her to seek out other girls who felt alone and needed a friend, like her. Perhaps by focusing on who Jesus is for her, Ashlyn could have moved past her own self-absorption to let the light of Christ shine into the lives of others. Resting and relying on him is the only way Ashlyn would be free to reach out to others in love.

LAST LOOK AND JOURNALING
As you read the verses below, consider the ways that Jesus is the perfect friend. If you viewed him this way instead of expecting your friends to be "Jesus," how would your relationship with him change?

Proverbs 18:24 | Luke 12:22–30 | John 15:13

....

....

....

....

....

....

....

....

....

....

....

....

....

....

....

....

....

....

....

....

At the beginning of middle school, Sonia was considered part of the popular group, although more on the fringe. The other girls set the pace and initiated the plans. Sometimes Sonia was included, other times not. Being at the mercy of whoever took charge and decided whether or not to invite her led to great insecurity and self-doubt for Sonia.

Insecurity turns some people into wallflowers, but Sonia went in the other direction. She constantly tried to do things to grab the other girls' attention. Though she didn't realize what she was doing, Sonia was trying to manipulate others to like her more so that she could be part of the group's core.

She did this in subtle ways, like bringing treats for the lunch table, being the first to post a picture collage for some-one's birthday, or making surprise "Welcome Home" banners after someone had been away. Sonia thrived on being the one to share bits of gossip as a way to draw more attention to herself. Everything she was doing seemed to work as she climbed her way up the social ladder. Sometimes, though, it was at the expense of a few girls she used in order to get "in" with the people she really wanted to associate with.

Life started to look up for Sonia, but a nagging discontent remained. There were always others who were more popular or got more attention. Even though she had become a leader in a sense, her every decision and opinion was a reflection of the girls she was trying to keep up with. So, if Denise didn't like someone or something, neither did Sonia. And if Caroline bought a certain item, Sonia had to have it too. Basically,

Sonia was a follower, willing to do whatever was necessary to be viewed at the top.

By her sophomore year, many kids at her school had started using drugs. But when word got out that Sonia and her friends were doing it too, people were surprised. They hadn't seemed like the type.

In all honesty, Sonia was scared to death. She knew drugs were dangerous and had never expected to use them. Apparently, though, something scared her more than drugs. That something was how her friends would view her if she didn't participate, and how that would affect her status within the group. So instead of rising to the occasion to be a true leader, Sonia caved in to the pressure to do what her friends thought was harmless and fun.

In the end, Sonia's middle school and high school years were spent bowing to the pressure to fit in, continually striving to be like whomever she was with. Never willing to take a stand or express her own opinion, Sonia relied on others' opinions to determine her next move. In an effort to be considered great, she sacrificed her own morals and values time and time again. The sad thing is that no one ever had the chance to love the true Sonia, or even to see who she was. For that matter, Sonia didn't know herself.

Now it is your turn to detect where the truth of the gospel is needed to change Sonia's heart and help her see how she is finding her identity in false gods.

REFLECTION TIME

1. What are the idols ruling Sonia?
2. List some of their effects on her life.
3. Why did she use drugs, even though they scared her and she knew it was wrong?
4. How could knowing that Jesus was great *for* her change her own quest for greatness?

5. When have you seen thoughts and actions like Sonia's in yourself?

6. If you believed your answer to #4, how would it keep you from being ruled by others' opinions, the pressure to fit in, or the need to elevate yourself?

TRUTH TIME

Sonia has spent years trying to be "somebody." Her desire for attention, popularity, and acceptance have literally ruled her, to the extent that she was willing to be somebody she wasn't and do things she knew were wrong.

Even before she caved in to using drugs, Sonia was doing things to win the approval of those she wanted to be like. Most people saw Sonia as the sweetest thing—always bringing treats and doing special things for people. But as we saw in chapter 2, our hearts are deeply sinful and deceptive, even to ourselves. From the outside, we may look "good" and put together, but, like Sonia, we may be so blinded to our idols that we don't realize our motives for what we do.

Do you know what it's like trying to get others to like you? Have you felt pressure to fit in? Have you done things you are ashamed of because you wanted to be accepted as part of the group? Have you ever done or said something you shouldn't have because you were worried about what others would think of you?

If so, you know how Sonia felt, and you also know how quickly the tide of opinion can change. One day "they" may like you and the next day you feel like a "nobody." What typically happens then is that you try harder, and the more you try to please others, the more you lose yourself.

This is what happened to Sonia. After so much time spent as a chameleon, her identity was lost. No wonder she felt so discontented. She'd based who she was on others' opinions and thus had easily succumbed to peer pressure.

Fear is often the root sin beneath the surrender to peer pressure. Peer pressure doesn't necessarily come in the form of friends "pressuring" you to do something. In fact, peer pressure doesn't have to be verbalized at all. Often it is simply your own heart's willingness to do whatever it takes to grab hold of the affirmation and approval you so deeply desire. Again, the idol drives the behavior.

In Sonia, we see a girl craving the spotlight, thinking it is where she will find her identity. But in striving to elevate herself, she turns away from the Source of her true identity, the Giver of her immeasurable worth. Only Jesus can give her the assurance and security that he has made her okay—more than okay! At the cross, Jesus secured for all time Sonia's right standing before God. And he has therefore stamped her, "Approved!"

Wrap your mind around this: The Roman governor Pontius Pilate was also ruled by other people's opinion and the desire to be great. So much so that he refused to stand up for an innocent man and instead yielded to pressure to have Jesus crucified.

Even so, God in his goodness can take our sin and use it for his ultimate glory. Jesus had to die because we, like Pilate and like Sonia, need rescuing from our sin. We too have hearts that bow down to false gods. We too become blind to our sin. And we too look for other things to give us worth and significance.

How different life could be for Sonia and for us if we lived as if Christ's full acceptance was the only thing that matters. The truth is, it is! Yet we continue to care more about what another insecure teenage girl or guy thinks about us, even though we have our Savior King calling us his beloved children. He gave to us everything that is good about himself, providing the most secure identity we could ever imagine.

LAST LOOK AND JOURNALING

As you read the verses below, note that finding true life in Christ drives out the desires of our wandering hearts. What do you need to believe about Christ so that walking by the Spirit appeals to you more than other things?

Galatians 2:20 | Galatians 5:16–24

Story 8
Drinking

Prom had been the subject of non-stop talk at school ever since spring break. At first, it centered around who was asking whom and in what creative ways the "asks" would happen. Then the conversations moved to finding dresses and forming groups for the pre- and post-prom plans. For many, this included talk of party buses and coed sleepovers, both providing ample opportunities for drinking.

Ella had been on party buses before without any alcohol present, but things were different now. She is a junior; almost all of her guy friends drink and many of the girls too. For prom, the guys are definitely planning to sneak alcohol onto the bus, so the big question is who will drink and who won't.

A few girls made pacts not to drink and to hold each other accountable. Others were ready to try it. They didn't care what the non-drinkers thought. Ella is caught in the middle.

At past events, it seemed as if those who drank had way more fun. So, if she were honest, she would have to admit that she wanted to join in this time. But she wrestled with the fact that underage drinking is wrong, and she would be the only one from her Bible study group who didn't agree to the no-drinking pact.

When the night of prom arrived, Ella had her date sneak alcohol from his flask into her Diet Coke without letting her friends see. She didn't particularly like the taste, but she did like how the slight buzz loosened her up. After that, she decided that she didn't want to miss out on the fun she could have for the rest of high school by worrying about what her abstaining friends thought. After all, wasn't high school supposed to be about doing what makes you happy, having fun, and creating memories?

The next weekend, Ella went to her first keg party. The weekends and summer that followed were spent going to parties and hanging out with a new, wilder group of friends. This new life meant lying to her parents, distancing herself from her Bible study friends, and suppressing her guilty conscience over doing what she knew was wrong. But Ella didn't have too much time to think about it because of all the fun she was having and cool people she was meeting.

All was well in Ella's world. Or was it?

Now it's your turn to detect where Ella has stopped believing the gospel and is looking for her life and identity outside Christ.

REFLECTION TIME
1. Where is happiness found for Ella?
2. Why are the partying and new friends more appealing to Ella than not drinking, and spending time with her former Bible study friends?
3. If Ella believes that what she is doing is wrong, why do you think she is still doing it?
4. What does Ella value most?
5. What temptations are most appealing to you?
6. How do you identify with the idols of Ella's heart?

TRUTH TIME
Everything seems great in Ella's world. She loves going to parties and socializing with new friends. But is it really all it appears to be?

Right now she would say yes, because she is happy and everything is going her way. Things are new and exciting, and the forbidden makes her feel older and more sophisticated. The fun she is having outweighs the guilt. Even leaving her old friends behind hasn't created much remorse. She is doing exactly what she wants to do.

For most who indulge in underage drinking, the desire is not just to enjoy a few sips over dinner with friends, but to get obliterated. They want to cut loose, lose their inhibitions, and perhaps attract attention from the opposite sex. The enjoyment Ella is getting from her choices is enough to make her unwilling to stop.

Her initial guilt subsided as the fun became more important. Leaving her old friends and convictions behind, she has turned away from God and toward these other things to give her significance.

Luke 12:34 tells us, "For where your treasure is, there will your heart be also." What matters most to Ella is her personal happiness and having fun. These treasures (or idols) have led her to indulge in what she knows is wrong, and she doesn't care.

It's the cotton candy illusion. The fluffy, pink spun sugar piled high on the stick looks so tasty and sweet, and it is. But when you bite on it, you discover that there isn't much there. It's not nearly as satisfying as it appeared. And, since there is absolutely no nutritional value, your health would rapidly decline if that's all you kept eating.

This is the path Ella is on. It's just not evident to her yet. The only way she will stop trying to live on cotton candy is to discover that it's not all it pretends to be.

Sometimes, like Ella, we grow indifferent to our sin and blind to our idols because everything is going well. God even permits this, sometimes for a long time, which reflects his patient, enduring love for his children. Sometimes it takes something bad or even traumatic to bring us back to reality and truth. Ultimately, the only way Ella will stop enjoying the partying is to see it for what it is—to see its emptiness and its inability to fill her, just like cotton candy.

In Hebrews we read of Moses, who "refused to be called the son of Pharaoh's daughter, choosing rather to be mistreated with the people of God than to enjoy the fleeting pleasures of sin" (Hebrews 11:24–25). The only reason Moses would give up a life of ease is because he considered a life with God a much greater treasure.

Seeing Christ as more worthy of our loyalty is the only way we will forsake the things that seem to offer such pleasure. We have to be more captivated by who Jesus is for us than we are by the cotton candy lie that life is found in having fun and being happy. At the end of the day, if our security and life are not bound up in him, we will keep chasing after things that will temporarily fill us but eventually leave us empty. We will spend a lifetime turning to false gods to give us the "happiness" rush we crave, only to discover that it takes something more.

The life we have in Christ does not promise that things will always go the way you want and make you happy. But life in Christ produces a joy you will never find apart from him, a joy that comes from knowing that you are his. He is for you and will never fail or forsake you. Even on the bad days, he is with you. This is what Moses discovered through the hardships in Egypt and the wilderness. This is what produced the faith to believe in things hoped for and not seen (Hebrews 11:1), and to believe that something greater was awaiting him than the temporary pleasures we often settle for.

Discovering these same truths is what will lead Ella away from her idols and back to Christ.

LAST LOOK AND JOURNALING

Evaluate your heart in light of the passages below. Where is your treasure? Do you yearn for something more, or do you look for life in the here and now? Journal your thoughts as to why the temporary pleasures of the world mean more than a life in Christ. Ask God to help you see and worship him as your greatest treasure.

1 John 2:15–17 | Colossians 3:1–2

Claire and Jackson live in the same neighborhood. They carpooled together from middle school until sophomore year, when they each got their licenses. At different times, one or the other had low-key crushes on the other, but nothing ever happened between them. Early on, Claire thought that if they dated and then broke up, it would be awkward. She decided she would rather not date Jackson than risk losing his friendship altogether. And as time went on, their friendship grew into a seemingly safe, brother-sister relationship.

Still, Claire felt a little possessive when her friends liked him, though she kept her feelings to herself. When he talked to her about which girl he should take to homecoming, it was the same thing.

She enjoyed being the one who knew what was going on with him, the one other girls came to for information about him. After all, he was one of the cutest guys in the school and she was the one he called to hang out with, to go for a run, or to ride together to football games. It made her feel special.

Without realizing it, Claire's association with Jackson had become part of her identity. He made her feel more important and popular. And being close friends with him gave her access to all of his friends. Often she was the only girl just hanging out with the cool, popular guys. Because of this added benefit, Claire would often bail on plans with her girlfriends so she could be with all the guys. Unbeknownst to Claire, Jackson was doing the same thing: enjoying the benefits of having a pretty, popular girl "friend" who connected him to other pretty, popular girls.

This pattern continued throughout most of high school. Then, one day, Jackson started liking an underclassman. All of a sudden, Claire was no longer the one he called. Claire couldn't believe that he liked this girl—she didn't seem to be his type at all! What made it worse was that her friends seemed to like her; they even encouraged Jackson to date her. When Claire kept picking the girl apart, her friends asked why she cared so much, if she didn't want to date Jackson anyway.

Why *did* she care so much? She asked herself that question, but she couldn't really explain how she felt. After a few weeks, she couldn't refrain from accusing him of dropping his friends, including her, because he was so smitten by this girl. Yes, he was preoccupied, but he certainly had not abandoned his friends. Only Claire believed that to be true. Something more was going on inside her. To get so upset and depressed over this did not make sense—unless it was because her view of herself was more tied up with Jackson than she'd ever realized. But what did it point to?

Now it is your turn to detect where Claire has built her identity and how God's Word needs to penetrate her heart.

REFLECTION TIME

1. What made Jackson's friendship so appealing to Claire?
2. Why does Claire react the way she does when Jackson finds a girlfriend?
3. What issues of idolatry and worth does Claire's reaction point to?
4. Why do you think it is difficult for a friendship to exist between a girl and a guy without one or the other using the other in some way for their benefit?

5. In what ways have you used friendships to give you a sense of worth?

6. When you realize that you are looking to other people to bring you significance and worth, what must you go back to?

TRUTH TIME

We were made for relationship. We were created in the image of God to be in fellowship with one another and to live for the good of others. Therefore, God declared in the garden of Eden that it was not good for man to be alone. It is also not good for us to live in isolation. Our desire for friendships is good.

But things go wrong when we turn a good thing into an ultimate thing. A good and legitimate desire for friends can easily become something we depend on to give us our identity. This happens when we turn to people as our source of significance and worth, as became the situation between Claire and Jackson.

How do you know whether your friendships are in their proper place? One good test is to consider which friends you want to be with and why. Have you chosen certain friends to hang out with because of the benefit they bring you? Do you feel more important if you are seen with them? Have you stopped hanging out with other people, not because you didn't have fun with them, but because they weren't very popular?

Certainly this is not what God intends for our relationships. As God's image-bearers, our friendships should reflect what we see in the Trinity, where God the Father, Jesus the Son, and the Holy Spirit revolve their lives around one another, seeking to elevate the other. This means that the real beauty of friendships is not what we get out of them, but what we give to them. In other words, our friendships should display Jesus in the way we seek to serve, love, uplift, care for, give to, invest in, and cherish one another. Had this been Claire and Jackson's view of friendship, instead of seeking to gain from each other, Claire would have been happy for Jackson in his new relationship and even sought to get to know his new girlfriend.

Instead, Claire's negative reaction to Jackson's girlfriend indicates that her relationship with Jackson was mostly about what *she* got out of it. It was hard for her to be happy for him when she had lost so much that she'd relied on for popularity and a good reputation. The fact that Jackson no longer pays attention to his long-term friendship with Claire indicates that he'd been operating much the same way. The benefits of being "close" to an opposite-sex friend are what had kept their friendship intact until now—for both of them.

They both had enjoyed each other, not necessarily for who they were, but because of what the other brought to them. Claire loved being connected to Jackson because he was cute and popular. The same could be said for Jackson's attraction to Claire—he enjoyed being seen with a pretty girl. But now that he has a girlfriend, he no longer "needs" Claire. And Claire has lost her inside connection, not just to Jackson, but to his friends.

Without knowing it, Claire's sense of worth had been attached to him. Being "in" with the guys and getting attention from both girls and guys because of her friendship with Jackson bolstered her self-esteem. When he no longer needed her for his own significance, she reacted in anger. It felt like her identity had been stripped away.

Claire needs to see how her friendship with Jackson had become an idol. She was relying on it to give her the attention, popularity, and importance she craved. The change in the friendship left her feeling lost. What she needs now is to see how she had turned to Jackson to give her what only God can give. She needs to be honest about how she had "used" their friendship. Often times it is the perks of a coed relationship that attract us to the friendship. Add in the likeliness of one or the other having romantic feelings, and the relationship becomes muddied with mixed motives and a lack of transparency.

Facing our idols is hard, but strong emotions can be a sign that we are holding tightly to something we think we must have. When this happens, we need to be willing to dig deeper to uncover why we feel the way we do. Once we can identify what we are turning to for life and identity, we can confess that to God and repent of trusting the idol that kept us from trusting him.

When Claire is able to do this, she will no longer feel resentful toward Jackson. She won't feel the need to tear down his girlfriend. She will be able to enjoy her friends for who they are, not for what they bring her, and she'll be more interested in loving them well. She will be able to remember that her significance is not based on her friends, but on the God who loves her so much that he came to earth to restore a relationship with her.

LAST LOOK AND JOURNALING

As you read the following verses, think about God's promises to you. How does hearing about his love and promises help reorient you back to truth?

Psalm 34:5 | Jeremiah 29:11 | John 15:9

. . . .

. . . .

. . . .

. . . .

. . . .

. . . .

. . . .

. . . .

. . . .
. . . .
. . . .
. . . .
. . . .
. . . .
. . . .
. . . .
. . . .
. . . .
. . . .
. . . .
. . . .
. . . .
. . . .
. . . .
. . . .
. . . .
. . . .
. . . .
. . . .

Maggie's world turned upside down when her parents divorced. She resented her dad for what he'd done to her mom. She was mad that they had to move out of their nice house and her mom had to take a full-time job. To help ease her mom's stress now that dad was gone and her sister away at college, Maggie took on most of the cooking and household chores. She also started babysitting more to pay for her clothes, gas, and what little social life she had time for. But along with the grown-up problems and responsibilities came a huge void. Maggie was lonely and sad.

She didn't want to burden her mom with her feelings and didn't think her friends would understand. She wanted a guy to make her feel special and give her the male attention she lacked from her dad. Seeking such attention led her to start dressing in a way she knew her mom would disapprove of. It was easy to hide, though. She left for school after her mom was already at work and returned home in workout clothes since her last class of the day was P.E. Plus, she did her own laundry.

Maggie liked the feeling she got from leading guys on and knowing they thought she looked "hot." Before long, though, she zeroed in on a boy named Chase. The flirtatious texting soon turned to talking and then moved to spending time with each other outside of school.

Maggie knew her mom didn't allow boys over when she wasn't home, but what her mom didn't know wouldn't hurt her. Besides, she didn't get why it should matter if they were just doing homework together. At least that's how she justified her behavior in her mind, though she was well aware of the perfect opportunity it created for Chase to make his first move on her.

What boy wouldn't seize the opportunity to be alone with an attractive, available girl? Maybe a few would be able to resist, but since sex is on the mind of most teenage boys most of the time, Chase and Maggie put themselves in a vulnerable situation and they both knew it.

Chase did exactly what Maggie was hoping for, and it was just a matter of time before these afternoon study sessions turned into regular hook ups. Maggie had always intended to wait for sex until marriage, but Chase was such a charmer! She wanted to keep him interested. To make it easier, she even went on birth control after convincing her mom that she needed to go to the dermatologist for help with her acne. That is, after all, how the other girls practiced safe sex without letting their parents know that they were sexually active.

As the months passed, Chase grew tired of Maggie demanding so much of his time. She always wanted him to be with her. She got jealous even if he was playing basketball with his guy friends. But every time he tried to break up with her, Maggie promised to change.

Their physical relationship never waned, but Maggie sensed Chase wasn't that into her anymore. Desperate to keep the relationship going, she tried harder and harder to hold onto him. But the more she clung, the greater the rift became. Her desperation only intensified the loneliness and sadness she'd felt before he came into her life. The same feelings of rejection she experienced after her dad left swept over her again. Where was God? Didn't he care about her, or had he abandoned her too?

Now it is your turn to detect where Maggie has stopped believing the truth of the gospel and is looking to false gods for identity and worth.

REFLECTION TIME

1. Why does Maggie feel a void in her life?
2. Whether she realizes it or not, how is she trying to fill that void?
3. What truths does she need to see and experience?
4. How would this insight help her to stop seeking from Chase what only God can give?
5. Where do you turn, other than God, to fill voids in your life?
6. If you believed your answer to #4, how would it help you to be satisfied in Christ alone?

TRUTH TIME

Maggie is thirsty for love, affection, and attention. Her dad has left the family and is rarely present in her life, and her mom is overwhelmed with a demanding job, single parenting, and her own personal grief and struggles after the divorce. What Maggie is not receiving from her parents she seeks from boys, specifically Chase.

While her parents' divorce is certainly a significant shaping influence on Maggie's life, the blame for Maggie's choices cannot simply be placed on her parents. Shaping influences, such as divorce, sickness, death, moving, financial changes, catastrophic events, and suffering, certainly affect us. We are also shaped by what our family is like, what they believe, and where we live. But none of these influences unilaterally determine how we think or what we say and do. God reigns over all of the uncontrollable circumstances in our lives, and how we think about him will shape the way we interpret everything else around us.

Even though she may be a Christian, Maggie has turned to Chase to fill her in ways only Jesus can. When Jesus calls us into relationship with himself, he wants us to bring him all of our needs, hurts, and emptiness so that he can fill us, strengthen us, and grow us. However, like Maggie, when we have been hurt, felt rejection, or suffered, our anger often is directed at God and he becomes the last person we want to draw near to. God is big enough, though, to listen to our honest cries. He already knows how we feel but calls us to pray our pain to him. As we learned in part 1, because Jesus came to earth and experienced all that we do, he knows what it's like. He can enter in to our every emotion. Sadly, it appears that Maggie stuffed her feelings and turned instead to a boy, looking to him to satisfy her in a way no human, even a husband, can do.

In her desire to be wanted and loved, she sacrificed her commitment to save sex for marriage. She gave Chase the precious gift of herself. Now a part of him will always be with her and a part of her with him. Sex powerfully connects us to another person in deep ways we barely understand. So when Chase pulled away, Maggie tried to hold on.

Sex is not nothing! So, whether you are tempted to give yourself to a boyfriend you intend to marry some day or to a "friend with benefits," stop! Remember that God designed sex to be a gift within heterosexual marriage for a reason.

Let's go back to Genesis 2, where Adam and Eve lived with each other "naked and unashamed." During sex, you are vulnerable and exposed, but within marriage this is an expression of the safety and freedom of being in Christ. There is no shame and nothing to hide. Outside of marriage, being exposed in such an intimate way carries with it a weight of shame. After giving herself to Chase to win his love, Maggie's shame led her to desperately try to hang on to him.

Maggie needs to go back to the cross to see a Savior who meets her in the midst of life's ups and downs. Hebrews 12:2 says it was ". . . for the joy that was set before him [that Jesus] endured the cross, despising the shame. . . ." Though Jesus was mocked, rejected, stripped, beaten, and left to hang naked on a cross, he considered it nothing compared to his reason for doing it—his love for his children.

Jesus died naked in order to clothe you with his righteousness. This is how he views you, PERIOD. So if you are living Maggie's story or carrying the weight of shame and guilt for another reason, there is only one place to go, and that is the cross. Bring your guilt to him and rest, knowing that his sacrificial death did everything necessary to make you pleasing, acceptable, and beautiful to him. He is the only one who can love you perfectly. As you embrace this truth, you can know that he has made you whole.

LAST LOOK AND JOURNALING

As you read the following passages, meditate on the truth that God not only took our shame to the cross, but he delights and rejoices in us! Do you believe this is true for you? If not, ask him to help you. Or spend time thanking him for his fierce love for you.

Isaiah 62:2–5 | Romans 8:38–39 | 2 Corinthians 5:17 | 1 Peter 2:24

. . . .

. . . .

. . . .

. . . .

. . . .

. . . .

. . . .

. . . .

. . . .

. . . .

Nora has grown up in a Christian home with a "good" family. Her parents have always taught Sunday school, volunteered with different charities, and been involved with various social organizations. It looks great, but what others perceive is very different from what Nora experiences at home.

She knows that they aren't the perfect family and that her parents aren't the model parents everyone thinks they are. In fact, Nora feels constantly slighted and hurt, watching them treat everyone else the way they do when she receives so little attention. No matter how obedient and respectful she is, it never seems to be enough to win their love. Their inattention makes her feel like something is wrong with her.

After years of feeling emotionally neglected, Nora has put up walls of protection that keep her from making close friends. Not that you would ever know it: Nora is friendly with everyone and appears happy. But she uses her witty sense of humor to hide the loneliness she really feels.

Working on the yearbook staff during her senior year, Nora, for the first time, began to truly connect with a female classmate over their similar quirkiness. As they began to spend time together outside of yearbook duties, Nora found herself thinking about Charlotte all the time. She loved the way Charlotte made her feel important. When she wasn't with her, she began feeling jealous of Charlotte's other friends. She had never felt like this before about anyone, and having such feelings for a girl scared her.

Could she be gay?

She knew this was wrong. All her life, homosexuality had been presented as a terrible sin. And even though society's views had changed, she could not begin to fathom what her parents would think if this were true of her. At the same time, the way she felt with Charlotte gave her hope that it was possible to experience love. Surely God wanted her to be happy!

Despite her fears and guilt, Nora decided it was worth experimenting. Charlotte made it clear that she was not interested in Nora that way, but she encouraged Nora to join the LGBTQ club at school. There she met students who told her that if she felt that way about a girl, she must be a lesbian. It was nothing to be ashamed of. Nora concluded that this must be the path she was meant to take. She did her best to squelch the guilt.

Now it is your turn to detect where Nora has stopped believing the gospel and is basing her identity on lies.

REFLECTION TIME

1. What does Nora desire most?
2. What made Charlotte so attractive to Nora?
3. On what is Nora basing her happiness?
4. How is Nora failing to trust that what God wants for her is best?
5. Is getting what you want always a good thing?
6. When you have had an unmet desire, how have you tried to fulfill it?

TRUTH TIME

All her life, Nora has lacked nurture and attention from her parents. Not knowing their love contributed to her insecurity, creating a deep thirst for affirmation and affection. She desperately craves to be known, but she fears rejection and feels unworthy at the same time. This has made relationships challenging.

When she and Charlotte started spending time together as friends, Nora liked having someone genuinely interested in her (not romantically, but as a friend). Since her family did not display such interest and care, she became enamored with Charlotte. As they continued spending time together, Nora's repressed desires bubbled to the surface and she became emotionally dependent on Charlotte's attention.

With these desires flaring up inside her, she was confused by what seemed like her crush on a girl. She didn't see clearly that it was having her desires met that felt so good. Nora's longings for attention, love, and connection are not wrong; they are legitimate desires of the human heart.

It is when our desires go against God's will or rule over us as a false god that they become sinful. This is why author and speaker Rosaria Butterfield says, "Homosexuality is con- sequential, not causal. Homosexuality is an identity-rooted ethical outworking of this: original sin."[4] In other words, homo- sexuality is an outworking of identity struggles rooted in our sinful nature. As with any other sin, we must see homosexuality as a pointer to something deeper going on inside us.

Nora's desires turned sinful when the need for affirmation from another human being (regardless of gender or romantic feelings) became greater to her than God's affirmation. This desire became a ruling desire that led her to pursue a lesbian relationship. To justify her decision, she reasoned that God would want her to be happy.

Perhaps she told herself that God wouldn't have given her those feelings only to deprive her of experiencing love. But as we saw in chapter 4, following Jesus as a disciple means finding life in him. To find our life, or identity, in him means forsaking finding life, meaning, security, or value in anything or anyone else. This means that we must die to our fleshly desires. The Christian life is, after all, a constant battle against temptation, against the things that entice us away from what God says is good. Like Eve, we easily fall for the lie that what we see (or feel, or believe) is what we must have at all costs. If we know this about ourselves, we can fight the continual battle against our fleshly desires and idolatrous ways. Acting on our desire for happiness at all costs is not for our good, and we must ask God to restrain us from evil. Similarly, dealing with same-sex attraction requires going to battle against the flesh with the help of the Holy Spirit.

We know from God's Word that God sets parameters for us not to withhold good from us, but to provide and protect. It may sound strange, but when it comes to sex, God wants us to enjoy the best sex possible! He created it for our pleasure within the context of marriage between a man and a woman. He designed male and female bodies to be uniquely different yet perfectly complementary. Not only do our bodies fit together physically, but our differing strengths and weaknesses are intended to enhance and complete one another too. All this is expressed within the covenant of heterosexual marriage.

Sex in any other context is outside God's protective bounds, whether homosexual or heterosexual. It leaves us exposed to hurt, guilt, disgrace, and disease. It is not that God wants to deprive you; he is guiding you to the best way to have an intimate relationship.

Nora is looking to be satisfied in something that will never satisfy. Her homosexual desires are no worse and no different from any other sinful desires. Any time our desires become idols, we believe we must have them to be content, whole, and happy. In essence, we are saying that God is not enough; we need something else to give us wholeness.

Nora is seeking to find her identity through the person who can give her the affirmation she so desperately wants. But what happens when that person—whether it is a girl or a guy—fails? If Nora bases her worth on what someone else thinks of her, her sense of personal value will rise or fall according to that other person. Her true identity gets lost.

Going down the path of sin to get what we want is never good. Romans 1 states that when human beings exchanged the truth about God for a lie and worshipped and served the created thing rather than the Creator, God "gave them up" (Romans 1:26) to do what they wanted. In letting people do as they wish, God is removing his restraining hand from the consequences for their sin.

We all think we want to be in control and to rule ourselves, but in choosing to freely enjoy their sinful desires, human beings were choosing God's wrath. In contrast, God calls us to live under his rule to experience his best. Living within his holy and perfect will provides true freedom within the boundaries he has ordained. There are times when our desires become distorted and we thirst after something besides him, but he pursues us, lavishing us with forgiveness and grace, reminding us of our permanent acceptance in him.

LAST LOOK AND JOURNALING

After reading the following verses, write a prayer asking God to help you see his boundaries as protection and his love as greater than your every desire.

Romans 12:1 | 1 Corinthians 6:19–20 | Ephesians 2:4–5 | 1 Peter 2:9

. . . .

. . . .

. . . .

. . . .

. . . .

. . . .

. . . .

. . . .

· ·
· ·
· ·
· ·
· ·
· ·
· ·
· ·
· ·
· ·
· ·
· ·
· ·
· ·
· ·
· ·
· ·
· ·
· ·
· ·

Harper vividly remembers the day at recess in fourth grade when a couple of girls made fun of the pants she was wearing. She never said anything to anyone about it, but she never wore those pants again either. And from then on, she felt insecure around those girls.

A few years later, when Harper was in middle school, a friend told her that the pastel-colored dress she planned to wear to the dance was going to wash her out if she didn't get a spray tan. Even though her friend said it jokingly, Harper's mind went back to that moment on the elementary school playground. Insecurity flooded her mind again. What her friend said must be true or she wouldn't have said it.

Harper began to wonder if everyone secretly joked about her pale skin. She hated feeling like a ghost, and her freckles and wavy red hair didn't help either. "Why did God make me like this?" she wondered. Now she didn't even want to go to the dance.

To add to her insecurities, most of her friends are good-looking, with bronzed skin and blonde hair. The things they talked about, whether it is fashion, makeup tips, or boys, made them seem so much more sophisticated than she. She felt like the little sister who never had anything to add to the conversation.

Increasingly, Harper began spending more time alone in her room, listening to music. It bothered her parents that she was shutting them out, no longer the vibrant, carefree girl she had always been. But when they asked her if something was bothering her, she always answered that she was okay. Finally they dropped it, hoping it was a normal teenage stage she would outgrow. But behind her closed bedroom door, Harper had found something else to bring her comfort.

The first time Harper took a razor blade to her arm, she was shocked that she had actually done it. Plagued with guilt and shame, she promised herself she wouldn't do it again. But she couldn't erase the image of the blood seeping out of her. As warped as it seemed, there was something beautiful about it that begged her to do it again.

The next time, as she made the clean straight slash across her arm, she felt more alive than she had in a long time. It was as if the emotional pain inside was being released, perhaps a rush much like a drug addict experiences. But once the temporary high was over, she needed to do it again. Soon self-harm became Harper's regular coping mechanism.

Now Harper had to constantly cover up, not just her arm but also any evidence that might be left behind in her room. The deceit added to the guilt she was working hard to deny. Cutting was a sweet release but, at the same time, she was sinking deeper into depression.

Now it is your turn to evaluate what is going on with Harper. Use the questions below to consider how she has stopped believing the gospel and how the gospel reaching her heart would change her situation.

REFLECTION TIME
1. What is Harper seeking to accomplish by cutting?
2. What is she not doing with her guilt and shame?
3. What lies does she believe about herself and about God?
4. What truths about God is she failing to believe?
5. What do you do with your guilt and shame?

6. What keeps you from immediately going to God with your guilt and shame?

TRUTH TIME

Harper has been hurt by the words of others. Those individuals probably don't even remember saying what they did and they would be surprised to know that their flippant comments from long ago continue to sting. While it is tempting to blame them for setting Harper on the course to self-harm, it is really her response to their words that is the shaping influence on her life.

Instead of brushing off the girls' catty comments, she accepted them as truth. But this supposed truth was really Satan's lie, telling her that she did not measure up to a standard of acceptability. She has allowed that lie to rule her instead of resting secure in who Christ says she is.

Do you see her idol? Do you see how it controls her?

Harper is seeking to find her identity in the approval of others—what they think of her—and making their acceptance more important than what God thinks. The more these idolatrous thoughts consume her heart and mind, the more depressed she has become. As is common with depression, Harper became numb to any emotion, so when she first cut herself and experienced pain, it felt good just to feel something. But as she went deeper into a pattern of self-harm, the temporary feeling of being alive was drowned out by the more lasting effects of guilt and shame.

Harper would tell you that she knows that what she is doing is wrong. Her shame about her cutting adds to her shame about her other perceived shortcomings. But she now finds cutting to be an almost irresistible form of release—it increases her self-hatred and eases her emotional pain at the same time. The thing she had hoped would set her free has instead enslaved her. The drawing of blood was like a form of sacrifice, or atonement, for her failures. (However, not everyone engaging in self-harm uses cutting as a form of punishment. For some, cutting is an outlet to release pain and the chance to simply feel something.)

Harper's cutting has made her more and more isolated from family, friends, and, most of all, Jesus. Though she is a believer, she has forgotten that Jesus's perfect life and sacrificial death meant that no one has the right to judge and condemn her when he has declared, "It is finished." She does not even have the right to judge and condemn herself! Jesus has declared that his children are forgiven, righteous, and beloved. Harper needs to hold onto those promises and let them shape her life and identity, instead of the rejection of others that has led her to reject herself.

Can you imagine how life would change for her if she really believed this?

If she believed these truths about God, she would know that because of Jesus, God makes none of the demands that come with living under the law (never mind the standards we set for ourselves). And when we fail to meet God's law—which is the only standard that really matters—there is always forgiveness and grace because Jesus met that perfect standard for us. The freedom Harper could find in resting in his love is something she will never find with cutting or self-harm. The more she practices them, the more enslaved she will be and the less relief they will provide.

If Harper rested in God's acceptance of her as an imperfect yet fully redeemed sinner, she wouldn't have to cut. She would live free of the chains of false standards that have bound her. She would flourish because, no matter what others said or thought about her, it wouldn't matter anymore. She would know the value of God's acceptance above all and embrace who he created her to be, pale skin and all.

LAST LOOK AND JOURNALING

Read the following verses and then journal about how you feel or act would change if you believed that your sin is completely atoned for and you have been set free.

Ephesians 1:7–12 | Ephesians 2:8–10 | Hebrews 10:19–23

. . . .
. . . .
. . . .
. . . .
. . . .
. . . .
. . . .
. . . .
. . . .
. . . .
. . . .
. . . .
. . . .
. . . .
. . . .
. . . .
. . . .
. . . .
. . . .
. . . .

Note to Self

BECAUSE OF WHO JESUS IS FOR ME, I AM . . .

Alive   "But God, being rich in mercy, because of the great love with which he loved us, even when we were dead in our trespasses, made us alive together with Christ—by grace you have been saved—and raised us up with him and seated us with him in the heavenly places in Christ Jesus . . ." Ephesians 5:4–6

Beautiful   "You are altogether beautiful, my love; there is no flaw in you." Song of Solomon 4:7

Blameless   "There is therefore now no condemnation for those who are in Christ Jesus." Romans 8:1

Blessed   "Blessed is the man who remains steadfast under trial, for when he has stood the test he will receive the crown of life, which God has promised to those who love him." James 1:12

Child of God   "But to all who did receive him, who believed in his name, he gave the right to become children of God . . ." John 1:12

Chosen   "But you are a chosen race, a royal priesthood, a holy nation, a people for his own possession, that you may proclaim the excellencies of him who called you out of darkness into his marvelous light." I Peter 2:9

Daughter of the King   ". . . and I will be a father to you, and you shall be sons and daughters to me, says the Lord Almighty." 2 Corinthians 6:18

Dearly Loved	"As the Father has loved me, so have I loved you. Abide in my love." John 15:9
Friend of God	"No longer do I call you servants, for the servant does not know what his master is doing; but I have called you friends, for all that I have heard from my Father I have made known to you." John 15:15
Heir of God	"And if children, then heirs—heirs of God and fellow heirs with Christ, provided we suffer with him in order that we may also be glorified with him." Romans 8:17
His Workmanship	"For we are his workmanship, created in Christ Jesus for good works, which God prepared beforehand, that we should walk in them." Ephesians 2:10
Known	"Before I formed you in the womb I knew you, and before you were born I consecrated you; I appointed you a prophet to the nations." Jeremiah 1:5
New Creation	"Therefore, if anyone is in Christ, he is a new creation. The old has passed away; behold, the new has come." 2 Corinthians 5:17
Purposeful	"For I know the plans I have for you, declares the Lord, plans for welfare and not for evil, to give you a future and a hope." Jeremiah 29:11
Radiant	"Those who look to him are radiant, and their faces shall never be ashamed." Psalm 34:5
Redeemed and Forgiven	"In him we have redemption through his blood, the forgiveness of our trespasses, according to the riches of his grace, which he lavished upon us, in all wisdom and insight making known to us the mystery of his will, according to his purpose, which he set forth in Christ as a plan for the fullness of time, to unite all things in him, things in heaven and things on earth." Ephesians 1:7–10
Righteous and Holy	"And to put on the new self, created after the likeness of God in true righteousness and holiness." Ephesians 4:24

Rooted and Built Up	"Rooted and built up in him and established in the faith, just as you were taught, abounding in thanksgiving." Colossians 2:7
Salt and Light	"You are the salt of the earth, but if salt has lost its taste, how shall its saltiness be restored? It is no longer good for anything except to be thrown out and trampled under people's feet. You are the light of the world. A city set on a hill cannot be hidden." Matthew 5:13–14
Wonderfully Made	"I praise you, for I am fearfully and wonderfully made. Wonderful are your works; my soul knows it very well." Psalm 139:14

Acknowledgments

This book was born out of the experience of walking alongside my teenage daughter in her battle with an eating disorder. So I want to first acknowledge her courage to come to me for help. Rebecca, thank you for not shutting me out, but allowing me and trusting me to help bear your burdens. During your journey there were some really bad, hard days, but I praise God for his faithfulness and for his ongoing work in and through you. You are amazing, as truly beautiful on the inside as the outside, and I have learned much about compassion and grace from you.

Thank you, next, to my husband Pete for continuing to offer your critique and insight to the endless stream of writing I toss at you. Once again, without your preaching and teaching, I would not only have nothing to write, but I would not have grown in my own understanding of the gospel and grace the way I have.

Thank you to everyone at New Growth Press, who has made book writing possible and the long process actually enjoyable. It is a blessing to feel like I have a team of people behind me and for me.

Thank you to all my family and friends who have prayed for me in this endeavor, shared the survey link essential to writing this book, and promoted my work to others long before it was even complete.

I especially want to thank The Turtles—Jennifer Daniels, Ashley Loeffler, Carissa Pereira, Kristi Pierce, Heather Sudbury and Downie Mickler (even though you weren't on our trip)—my closest group of college friends who allowed me the time on our Bahamian vacation to finish the proposal for this book. While I pecked away on my iPad at the beach, you encouraged me to keep at it. You continue to be some of my biggest cheerleaders in my writing endeavors.

To my friends at Rooted Ministry, thank you for providing a platform for me to write and speak further about the truths of who Jesus is for us, and who we are in him. And Jessica Thompson—to you I am grateful for your willingness to write the Foreword to this book. Your consistent message of grace in the gospel is what we all need to hear more of all the time.

Lastly, I want to thank all of the teenagers from across the country who filled out my survey with honest answers and input. The information I was able to pull from them was truly beneficial to discerning the direction of this book and the stories that needed to be crafted. While all stories in this book are fictitious, they are realistic because of the behind-the-scenes peek I have been given into the world of teens.

Endnotes

1. "Behind the Scenes of a Selfie Society for Teens" is the survey for teen girls created by the author for this book's research.

2. From the hymn, "Turn Your Eyes upon Jesus," by Helen Howarth Lemmel, 1922.

3. Paul David Tripp, *Instruments in the Redeemer's Hands: People in Need of Change Helping People in Need of Change* (Phillipsburg, NJ: P & R Publishing, 2002), 85–86.

4. Rosaria Butterfield, "Homosexuality and the Christian Faith," https://www.youtube.com/watch?v=DVOWfUitLx8.